HIKING
ARIZONA II

by

Don R. Kiefer

GOLDEN
WEST ☼
PUBLISHERS

Cover photo: Aravaipa Creek by Dick Dietrich

All trail maps drawn by Robyn Wasserman

Library of Congress Cataloging-in-Publication Data
Kiefer, Don R.
    Hiking Arizona II / by Don Kiefer.
    Includes index.
    1. Hiking—Arizona—Guidebooks. 2. Arizona— Guidebooks.
    I. Title
GV199-42.A7K55 1993
917.91'0433—dc20   93-18100
ISBN 0-914846-70-1   CIP

Printed in the United States of America

Golden West Publishers
4113 N. Longview
Phoenix, AZ 85014, USA
(602) 265-4392

Dedication

I dedicate this book to my son, Monte A. Kiefer, who, although he is not with me in body on my hikes, is certainly with me in spirit.

I like having him along and, as a result, I never hike alone.

Acknowledgment

I almost feel guilty when I am called the author of a book. Perhaps I put it all together, but a lot of people have made it possible for me to do so. I would like to thank these people and organizations.

EVELYN LONG, Gilbert, Arizona, who started working with me back in 1986, my early newspaper days, and still transforms my presentations to her into the obvious works of art.

MESA TRIBUNE, Mesa, Arizona, who gave me the chance to learn and go public with my fascination for the great outdoors.

ROBYN WASSERMAN, Vail, Arizona, who has become a good friend of mine, and who has pushed her magic pen to create these maps and drawings for your use, and also to make this book possible.

KENNETH WARD, DICK HIGDON and LARRY MUTTER, who also have hiked with sore feet right along with me.

JOE MAIERHAUSER, lease owner and general manager of Colossal Cave Mountain Park, Tucson, Arizona, for his encouragement and his "you can do it" attitude on anything it took to make this book a reality.

Thanks also to the following:

Maricopa Parks and Recreation Department, Sedona Ranger District, Verde Ranger District, Bureau of Land Management, Santa Catalina Ranger District, Catalina State Park, City of Phoenix Parks Recreation and Library, Organ Pipe National Monument, Saguaro National Monument West, Saguaro National Monument East and Peaks Ranger District.

Thanks again for all your help.

ARIZONA AREA MAP

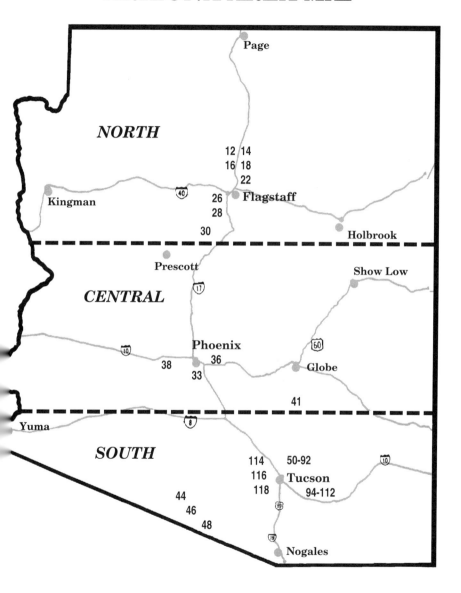

Page

NORTH

12 14
16 18
22
Kingman   40   26   Flagstaff
28
30   Holbrook

Prescott

Show Low

CENTRAL   17

Phoenix   50
10   38   36   Globe
33
41

Yuma   8

SOUTH   114   50-92
116   Tucson
118   94-112
44
46   86
48
19
Nogales

Trail Information begins on pages as listed above

Contents

(Continued on next page)

(Contents continued from previous page)

Introduction

ARIZONA! What would it be like to hike it all? We will never know; one's life span was not designed to allow enough time for any one man or woman to accomplish this. All we can hope for is that our minds get sprinkled with what information is available, due to people like you and me who will pay the dues to go just one more mile or around one more bend.

This book however will provide you with a tool, if used properly, that will move you closer to having "hiked it all."

Get ready to either enjoy, or tolerate, the lowland deserts. They make up an area soft with fresh scents, the gentle buzzing of the bees and the silent wanderings of the butterflies. The desert's other side is the extreme heat, many venomous creatures, and storms more vicious than you can imagine.

Also prepare yourself for high altitudes and, yes, even true tundra conditions right here in Arizona. There are areas so quiet you will think you have lost your hearing, with visibility beyond what you thought you could ever see, and so remote you will wonder if there is a way home. Of course, the other extreme exists here as well: snowstorms any day of the year, so much static electricity in the air that your clothes will crack with each step making it sound as if you are walking on potato chips, 50 m.p.h. winds being normal—Mother Nature on a bad day—and creatures that outweigh you three and four times that hopefully just watch you go by.

Perhaps you should just stay home; it's a good idea if you are planning to go unprepared. However, if you would like to experience and enjoy the wonders of Arizona, please acquaint yourself with every chapter in this book. Most of all, know and obey your own limitations.

Don R. Kiefer

Reading Trail Signs

"How elementary!" You may say. When you come upon a sign that reads "Peach Springs - 2.5 miles," how hard can it be to understand? Let's consider this, however. You get caught in a snowstorm and it dumps about four inches of snow and the terrain becomes level (it happened to me). Except for distance, the above trail sign is of no more value; it is obvious that you need to look for other trail signs besides a post and a board.

1. Chevrons

Chevrons are metal tabs about three inches square, that are tacked to trees along the trail about six to eight feet above the ground. The ones I have seen have been white, orange or red. You must be careful not to lose sight of the one you just passed before the next one comes into view. Some trees will have two chevrons indicating either that another trail connects the trail you are on, or that there is a very sharp turn in your trail. Take a minute to study the area well when two chevrons are encountered. Chevrons are found mostly in high altitudes.

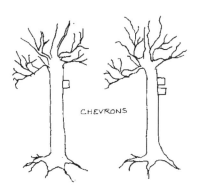

2. Tree Notches

These notches are carved into trees at about the five to six-foot level. Most are about 3/4 inch deep and have rounded edges because of the tree's ability to eventually heal over the notch. They are a little harder to spot as they take on the same color as the tree. Notches sometimes are found in the lower altitudes as well. They are interpreted exactly the same as chevrons.

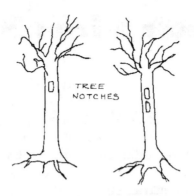

TREE NOTCHES

3. Cairns

Cairns are very expertly arranged stacks of rocks along the trail, graduating from a large base to almost a point. I have seen them from ten inches high to four feet high, and they simply guide your way. These are found on areas of trails that are just rock surfaces, where a path will never be worn and there are no trees for chevrons or notches. Believe me, it's a very hit-and-miss situation getting through areas like this without a scattering of rock cairns.

As you can see, trail signs come in many forms and it is a good idea to train yourself to spot them, even though you may not be having any problems finding your way.

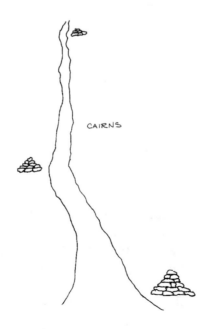

CAIRNS

Hiking Burn Areas

Since you are permitted to hike in burn areas, I felt it was prudent to pass along the following information, touching on not only your responsibilities but dangers as well.

1. Responsibilities

A recent burn area is very fragile. Although a burn area is nothing new (it's been going on since time began), we must still concern ourselves with its recovery.

Never enter a burn area until permitted, and never leave the trail or make any shortcuts. These areas are very susceptible to washouts which could be caused by new footprints off trail due to the burnout of the plants' root systems. One must take extra care with mountain bikes and horses as well. The plant life is also a real consideration as it will never be any more fragile than it is now.

If we all work together, the burn area will have a much faster recovery.

2. Dangers

A main concern, of course, is whether you still can actually follow the trail, due to trail notches on the trees being burned as well as wooden trail signs. Never hike a burn area without a thorough understanding of your topo map.

Another danger is roots and stumps that were already dead when the fire started and have completely burned away but not yet caved in. Roots leave a perfect hidden depression where you could twist or break an ankle. Also off trail are the stumps that have burned away leaving giant hidden holes, sometimes three to four feet deep, that could still contain hot coals in the bottom because of ash being such a good insulator.

If care is taken in a burn area, it can be a learning experience for the entire family. On the other hand, if you are careless and take chances, your outing may end in tragedy.

INNER BASIN TRAIL

ATTRACTION: This is a trip into the heart of an old volcano equal to Mt. Saint Helens with flows still visible.

REQUIREMENTS: 6 hours round trip; food, water, rain gear, map, waterproof shelter

LOCATION: San Francisco Peaks, Flagstaff

DIFFICULTY: Moderate

ELEVATIONS: 8600'-10,000'

LENGTH: 2 miles one way

MAPS REQUIRED: Humphreys Peak Quadrangle, 7.5 minute topographic, Coconino County

PERMIT : No

BIKES : No

EQUESTRIAN : Not permitted in the Inner Basin

WATER: Best to bring your own

INFORMATION: No camping in Inner Basin or above tree line. You must stay on the trail above tree line.

FIREARMS: Not restricted, but there is absolutely no need for a gun

PETS ON LEASH: Not in Inner Basin; elsewhere on leash only

TRAIL INFORMATION

From Flagstaff, drive north on US 89 for 12.5 miles to Forest Road 552, just past the Sunset Crater turnoff. Drive west on F.R. 552, bear left at the Lockett Meadow sign (about 1 mile), and continue to the trailhead. This dirt road may not be passable in early spring due to snow. You will have ample parking at Lockett Meadow, a good camping area.

Hiking toward the Inner Basin is southwest on an old road for about 1.5 miles, to the actual opening of the Inner Basin at the watershed cabins. You will find several routes into the basin to complete your hike. It is truly awesome being in an old volcano.

Remember, day use only, no overnight camping allowed in the Inner Basin at all.

INNER BASIN TRAIL

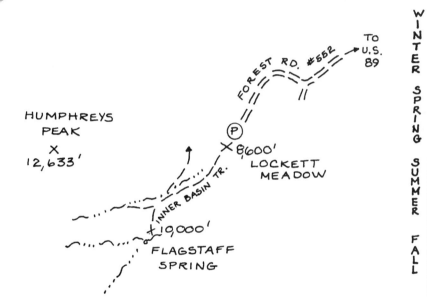

HUMPHREYS
PEAK
X
12,633'

TO
U.S.
89

FOREST RD. #552

P

X 8,600'
LOCKETT
MEADOW

INNER BASIN TR.

+ 10,000'
FLAGSTAFF
SPRING

WINTER SPRING SUMMER FALL

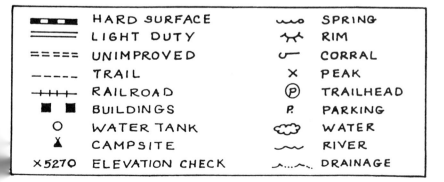

▰▱▰	HARD SURFACE	∽o	SPRING
═══	LIGHT DUTY	⋀⋀	RIM
=====	UNIMPROVED	⌣	CORRAL
-----	TRAIL	✕	PEAK
++++	RAILROAD	Ⓟ	TRAILHEAD
■ ■	BUILDINGS	P.	PARKING
O	WATER TANK	☁	WATER
▲	CAMPSITE	∼	RIVER
✕5270	ELEVATION CHECK	∼...∼	DRAINAGE

ABINEAU TRAIL

ATTRACTION: A lot of wildlife, abundance of colors in the fall, nice views of Grand Canyon and Painted Desert

REQUIREMENTS: 2.5 hours one way; food, water, rain gear, map, waterproof shelter

LOCATION: San Francisco Peaks, Flagstaff

DIFFICULTY: Moderate

ELEVATIONS: 8800'-10,400'-9800'

LENGTH: 3.8 miles one way

MAPS REQUIRED: White Horse Hills Quadrangle, 7.5 minute topographic, Coconino County; Humphreys Peak Quadrangle, 7.5 minute topographic, Coconino County

PERMIT : No

BIKES : No

EQUESTRIAN : Yes

WATER: Best to bring your own

INFORMATION: This trail, coupled with Bear Jaw Trail, makes a very nice loop hike

FIREARMS: Not restricted, but there is absolutely no need for a gun

PETS ON LEASH: Not in Inner Basin; elsewhere on leash only

TRAIL INFORMATION

From Flagstaff, take US 89 north for 14 miles to Forest Road 418. Go west on F.R. 418 for 7 miles to F.R. 9123J (about one mile west of Reese Tank). Go south on F.R. 9123J for 1.2 miles to the trailhead. The Abineau and Bear Jaw Trails begin at this point.

Abineau Trail climbs south up Abineau Canyon towards an old road connecting Abineau and Bear Jaw Trails. It is a very steady, steep climb. The trail travels through aspen and, towards the end, many ground-hugging tundra plants. This is the most likely location for bear in the area. Beware!

Bearing left on this old road, you will come to a "T" in the trail at 3.8 miles where Abineau Pipe Line Trail goes to the right or south, and, to continue your loop hike, take Bear Jaw Trail to your left.

ABINEAU TRAIL

1   0   1 MILE

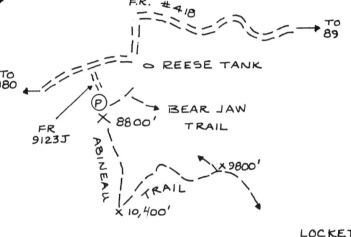

F.R. #418

TO
89

TO
180

⊙ REESE TANK

Ⓟ

FR
9123J

X 8800'

BEAR JAW
TRAIL

ABINEAU

TRAIL

X 9800'

X 10,400'

LOCKETT
MEADOW

W I N T E R   S P R I N G   S U M M E R   F A L L

X 12,633'
HUMPHREY'S
PEAK

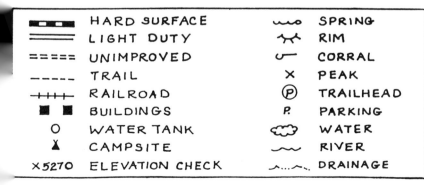

	HARD SURFACE		SPRING
	LIGHT DUTY		RIM
=====	UNIMPROVED		CORRAL
-----	TRAIL	×	PEAK
+++++	RAILROAD	Ⓟ	TRAILHEAD
▪ ▪	BUILDINGS	P.	PARKING
O	WATER TANK		WATER
▲	CAMPSITE		RIVER
×5270	ELEVATION CHECK		DRAINAGE

BEAR JAW TRAIL

ATTRACTION: A lot of wildlife, abundance of fall colors, nice views of Grand Canyon and Painted Desert

REQUIREMENTS: 2 hours one way; food, water, rain gear, map, waterproof shelter

LOCATION: San Francisco Peaks, Flagstaff

DIFFICULTY: Moderate

ELEVATIONS: 9800'-8800'

LENGTH: 2 miles one way

MAPS REQUIRED: White Horse Hills Quadrangle, 7.5 minute topographic, Coconino County; Humphreys Peak Quadrangle, 7.5 minute topographic, Coconino County

PERMIT : No

BIKES : No

EQUESTRIAN : Yes

WATER: Best to bring your own

INFORMATION: This trail, coupled with Abineau Trail, makes a very nice loop hike

FIREARMS: Not restricted, but there is absolutely no need for a gun

PETS ON LEASH: Not in Inner Basin; elsewhere on leash only

TRAIL INFORMATION

From Flagstaff, take US 89 north for 14 miles to Forest Road 418. Go west on F.R. 418 for 7 miles to F.R. 9123J (about 1 mile west of Reese Tank). Go south on F.R. 9123J for 1.2 miles to the trailhead. The Abineau and Bear Jaw Trails begin at this point.

This trail information will start with the thought in mind that you have already climbed Abineau Trail and arrived at this point. (Read your Abineau Trail information.) As you make your left turn onto Bear Jaw Trail be sure to soak up your view of the Grand Canyon, the split in the earth to the north.

Again the tundra plants are present, along with the aspens, as you make your way downhill, descending only about 500' per mile. This is a colorful area most of the year. The ever-present possibility of bear in this area is also high. Beware!

Soon you will arrive at Abineau and Bear Jaw trailheads, completing a loop hike.

BEAR JAW TRAIL

0   ½   1 MILE

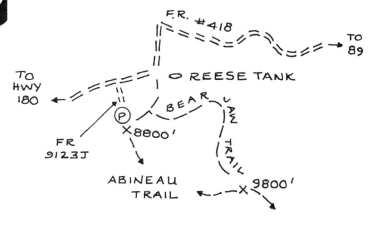

F.R. #418

TO 89

TO HWY 180 ←

O REESE TANK

BEAR JAW TRAIL

(P)

X 8800'

FR 9123J

ABINEAU TRAIL ←

X 9800'

LOCKETT MEADOW

HUMPHREYS PEAK   X 12,633'

W I N T E R   S P R I N G   S U M M E R   F A L L

▬▬▭▬ HARD SURFACE	∿o	SPRING
═══ LIGHT DUTY	⋏⋏	RIM
═════ UNIMPROVED	⌒	CORRAL
╶╴╴╴╴ TRAIL	X	PEAK
┼┼┼┼ RAILROAD	(P)	TRAILHEAD
■ ■ BUILDINGS	P.	PARKING
O WATER TANK	☁	WATER
▲ CAMPSITE	∿	RIVER
X5270 ELEVATION CHECK	∿...∿.	DRAINAGE

HUMPHREYS PEAK TRAIL

San Francisco Peaks

ATTRACTION: Mt. Humphreys is a unique geological feature illustrating the process of volcanism. This hike also presents a challenge in high altitude hiking and soon you will know if you are capable of any higher peaks.

A chance to view the San Francisco Peaks' groundsel (*Senecio franciscanus*), a small plant growing nowhere else in the world.

Here you can stand on the highest real estate in Arizona, as well as the only tundra conditions in the state.

After you sign in at the top, relax and see how many points of interest you can identify from your vantage point; they are just endless.

REQUIREMENTS: 8 hours round trip; food, water, rain gear, map, waterproof shelter

LOCATION: San Francisco Peaks, Flagstaff

DIFFICULTY: Difficult; know your limits and obey them

ELEVATIONS: 9590'-12,633'

LENGTH: 8.7 miles round trip

MAPS REQUIRED: Humphreys Peak Quadrangle; 7.5 minute topographic, Coconino County

PERMIT : No

BIKES : No

HUMPHREYS PEAK TRAIL

0   ½   1 MILE

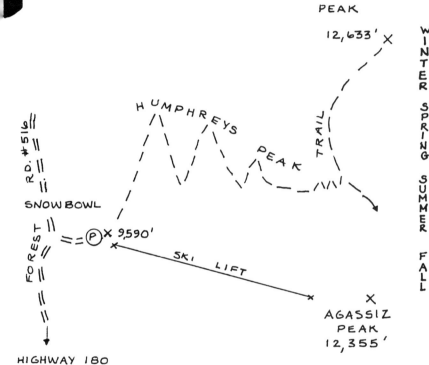

TRUE NORTH

WINTER SPRING SUMMER FALL

HUMPHREYS PEAK

12,633' X

HUMPHREYS PEAK TRAIL

RD. #516

SNOW BOWL

(P) X 9,590'

FOREST

SKI LIFT

X
AGASSIZ PEAK
12,355'

HIGHWAY 180

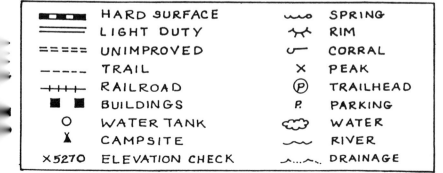

▬▫▬	HARD SURFACE	⌒⌒o	SPRING
═	LIGHT DUTY	⋎⋏	RIM
=====	UNIMPROVED	∽	CORRAL
-----	TRAIL	✕	PEAK
++++	RAILROAD	(P)	TRAILHEAD
■ ■	BUILDINGS	P.	PARKING
○	WATER TANK	☁	WATER
⅄	CAMPSITE	∼∼	RIVER
✕5270	ELEVATION CHECK	∼...∼	DRAINAGE

EQUESTRIAN : No

WATER: Best to bring your own

INFORMATION: All of the laws and regulations pertaining to wilderness apply on the peaks. Remember the elevation changes and steepness of the routes. On the upper slopes, the wind can be severe; winds over 50 mph are common. Pacific cold fronts with accompanying rain or snow can move in very quickly. Get to a safe area before the storm hits. A forested area away from ridge tops, ledges or rock outcrops, and tallest trees is the safest place to be.

This trail is not on your topo map but it should be taken anyway for reference (trail was constructed after the current topo map was revised).

Do not underestimate the thin air on this peak; you would be wise to prepare for this hike by hiking 8000' to 9000' peaks first.

A call to the airport at Flagstaff (602-774-3301) will give you the latest weather information. Patches of snow may remain into July. Violent electrical storms occur almost daily during July, and frequently during other spring, summer and fall months on these high mountains. Warning: hikers may find their hair standing on end and their clothing aglow with static electricity.

Once you reach the 11,400-foot elevation, you are near timberline. Stunted Englemann spruce and small bristlecone pines can be seen.

Camping is not allowed above 11,000-foot elevation or within the Inner Basin.

Hiking above timberline is restricted to designated trails only. Indiscriminate cross-country hiking is prohibited.

At 12,633 feet, Humphreys Peak is the highest point in Arizona. This small region in the San Francisco Peaks (eroded volcanic cones) is the only place in Arizona where tundra conditions exist.

FIREARMS: Not restricted, but there is absolutely no need for a gun nor its extra weight on a hike this difficult

PETS ON LEASH: On leash only

TRAIL INFORMATION

To get to the trailhead from Flagstaff, drive north on US 180 for

Continued next page

Humphreys Trail view. Note sign regarding "fragile tundra".

7 miles to F.R. 516, the Snow Bowl Road. Drive 7.4 miles on this paved road to the lower parking lot of the Snow Bowl facility. The trailhead is located at the north end of the parking lot.

This hiking experience cannot be matched by any other in the state. After leaving parking lot and continuing past the upper lodge, the trail actually parallels the ski tram for a short distance. This is as good a place as any to use discipline in order to pace yourself, which is mandatory on a trail this steep and high. Already steep, the trail now continues away from the ski lift (NE) as it starts a series of long switchbacks, and travels through aspens along the way. As the switchbacks get shorter and the trail steepens, you will have escaped the treeline and windy conditions are sure to be present (50 mph are common).

When you reach the saddle between Humphreys and Agassiz, you must not, for any reason, hike over to Agassiz Peak; it is off limits. This is a good place to take stock of how you feel before continuing the last mile or so to the peak (left turn); this last mile requires one solid hour of travel. However, for those of you that make it to the top, the views will be fantastic as you sit on the throne of Arizona. Sign the register and return the way you came.

WEATHERFORD TRAIL

ATTRACTION: A chance to view the San Francisco Peaks' groundsel (*Senecio franciscanus*), a small plant growing nowhere else in the world.

Fine views of Oak Creek Canyon and the Verde Valley from areas along the trail.

An alternate way to Humphreys Peak Trail; add one mile for this. Although longer, Weatherford Trail is not as demanding as Humphreys Peak Trail.

REQUIREMENTS: 11 hour round trip; food, water, rain gear, map, waterproof shelter

LOCATION: San Francisco Peaks, Flagstaff

DIFFICULTY: Moderate to difficult

ELEVATIONS: 8800'-12,020'

LENGTH: 8.7 miles one way

MAPS REQUIRED: Humphreys Peak Quadrangle; 7.5 minute topographic, Coconino County

PERMIT : No

BIKES : No

EQUESTRIAN : Not above Doyle Saddle

WATER: Best to bring your own

INFORMATION: All of the laws and regulations pertaining to wilderness apply on the peaks.   Remember the elevation changes and steepness of the routes. On the upper slopes, the wind can be severe; winds over 50 mph are common. Pacific cold fronts with accompanying rain or snow can move in very quickly. Get to a safe area before the storm hits. A forested area away from ridge tops, ledges or rock outcrops, and tallest trees is the safest place to be.

Do not underestimate the thin air in this area; you would be wise to prepare for this hike by hiking 8000' to 9000' peaks first.

A call to the airport at Flagstaff (602-774-3301) will give you the latest weather information. Patches of snow may remain into July. Violent electrical storms occur almost daily

WEATHERFORD TRAIL

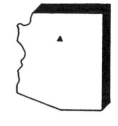

1   0   1 MILE

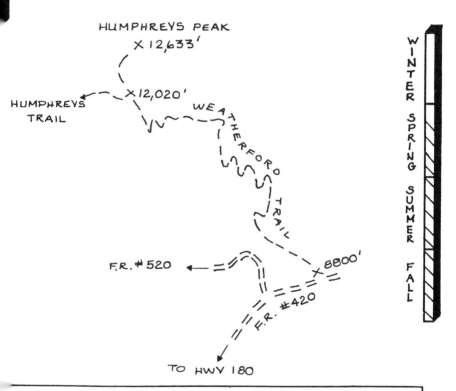

HUMPHREYS PEAK
X 12,633'

X 12,020'

HUMPHREYS
TRAIL

WEATHERFORD TRAIL

F.R. #520

X 8800'

F.R. #420

TO HWY 180

WINTER SPRING SUMMER FALL

	HARD SURFACE		SPRING
	LIGHT DUTY		RIM
=====	UNIMPROVED		CORRAL
-----	TRAIL	X	PEAK
++++	RAILROAD	(P)	TRAILHEAD
■ ■	BUILDINGS	P.	PARKING
O	WATER TANK		WATER
▲	CAMPSITE		RIVER
X5270	ELEVATION CHECK		DRAINAGE

during July, and frequently during other spring, summer and fall months on these high mountains. Warning: hikers may find their hair standing on end and their clothing aglow with static electricity.

Once you reach the 11,400-foot elevation, you are near timberline. Stunted Englemann spruce and small bristlecone pines can be seen.

Camping is not allowed above 11,400-foot elevation or within the Inner Basin.

Hiking above timberline is restricted to designated trails only. Indiscriminate cross-country hiking is prohibited.

FIREARMS: Not restricted, but there is absolutely no need for a gun nor its extra weight on a hike this difficult

PETS ON LEASH: On leash only

TRAIL INFORMATION

To reach the trailhead, follow US 180 north to Forest Road 420, Schultz Pass Road. Bear left at the intersection with Forest Road 557. Continue on Forest Road 420 for 6 miles to the trailhead. Forest Road 420 is a dirt road beyond the Forest Road 557 intersection. You will find parking on the south side of the road near the tank; actual trail starts north of Schultz Pass Road. Trail is an old road that led to Humphreys Saddle. Any vehicle traffic has been banned. The trail winds and gently climbs for about 5.1 miles to Doyle Saddle at not quite 11,000', and is easy to follow. It's interesting to notice the changing plant life as you gain altitude. Your first lookout is from here into the Inner Basin, the actual mouth of a dormant volcano. In another 1.8 miles, at approximately 11,200', will be Fremont Saddle. Some long switchbacks are now encountered as you skirt Agassiz Peak for the next 1.5 miles to the saddle between Agassiz and Humphreys with only .3 mile to go to the junction with Humphreys Trail.

If you do want to continue to Humphreys Peak on Humphreys Trail, it is a very grueling mile requiring one hour one way. Under no circumstances should you hike on over to Agassiz Peak; it is off limits.

You never know <u>who</u> you're going to meet on the trail!

Lockett Meadow at Inner Basin trailhead.

VULTEE ARCH TRAIL

ATTRACTION: A natural arch made out of sandstone; makes a fine day hike for the family

REQUIREMENTS: 1.5 hours one way; snack, water, rain gear, map

LOCATION: Red Rock-Secret Mountain Wilderness-Sterling Canyon—Lost Wilson Mountain, N.W. Sedona

DIFFICULTY: Easy

ELEVATIONS: 4820'-5220'

LENGTH: 1.7 miles one way

MAPS REQUIRED: Wilson Mountain Quadrangle, 7.5 minute topographic

PERMIT : No, but do realize it is wilderness area

BIKES : No

EQUESTRIAN : Yes

WATER: Not dependable, carry your own

INFORMATION: Road to trailhead is okay for a car if you take your time, although not recommended in wet weather

FIREARMS: Yes

PETS ON LEASH: Yes

TRAIL INFORMATION

To reach the trailhead, take Dry Creek Road from Highway 89A in West Sedona. Two miles north, turn right on Road #152. This road is rough but usable for passenger vehicles (not recommended during wet weather.) About 4.3 miles up this road you will reach a small, sandy opening or turnaround. Park and proceed hiking out the east end of the opening along a short jeep trail which dead ends at a drainage. Continue on footpath up the canyon.

This is an easy hike up Sterling Canyon with little elevation gain. Although it is a dry drainage most of the year with the possibility of hot temperatures, there is shade.

At about the halfway point, check out the sandstone cliffs on the right side, a spectacular sight. When you come to sandstone benches and a plaque, you are at trail's end. The plaque is in memory of Gerard and Sylvia Vultee who were killed in a plane crash near here in 1938. On the north side of the canyon is Vultee Arch.

VULTEE ARCH TRAIL

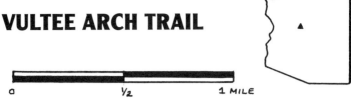

0   ½   1 MILE

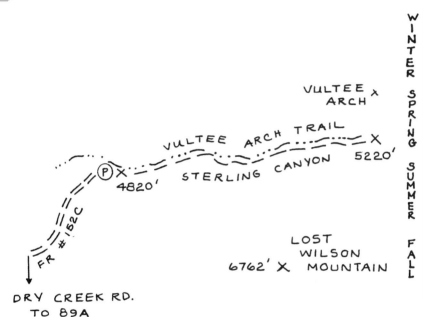

▬▬▬	HARD SURFACE	ᘉᘉ○ SPRING
═══	LIGHT DUTY	⋏⋏⋏ RIM
═════	UNIMPROVED	᠓ CORRAL
------	TRAIL	✕ PEAK
┼┼┼┼	RAILROAD	Ⓟ TRAILHEAD
■ ■	BUILDINGS	P. PARKING
○	WATER TANK	☁ WATER
▲	CAMPSITE	ᗐ RIVER
✕5270	ELEVATION CHECK	ᗐ....ᗐ DRAINAGE

DEVIL'S BRIDGE TRAIL

ATTRACTION: Trail ends at a natural red sandstone bridge; a fine day hike

REQUIREMENTS: 45 minutes one way; snack, water, rain gear, map

LOCATION: Red Rock-Secret Mountain Wilderness just north of Capitol Butte, N.W. Sedona

DIFFICULTY: Difficult

ELEVATIONS: 4610'-4950'

LENGTH: 1 mile one way

MAPS REQUIRED: Wilson Mountain Quadrangle, 7.5 minute topographic

PERMIT : No, but do realize it is wilderness area

BIKES : No

EQUESTRIAN : Yes

WATER: Not dependable, carry your own

INFORMATION: Road to trailhead is okay for a car except the last .4 mile. If in low-clearance vehicle, park and proceed on foot

FIREARMS: Gun

PETS ON LEASH: Yes

TRAIL INFORMATION

To reach the trailhead, take Dry Creek Road from Highway 89A in West Sedona; 2 miles north, turn right on Road #152. About 1.5 miles from the pavement, turn right onto a dirt road and park, if in a low vehicle. Follow the road to the turnaround. Road #152 is not recommended when wet.

Although a short hike, your work is cut out for you on your way to a spectacular sandstone arch. If in a passenger car, it will be necessary to hike about one-half mile to the turnaround and the trail. Some shade is to be enjoyed as you work your way to the arch that remains hidden until you are almost on top of it, so to speak.

At the bottom, the trail splits as one fork takes you to the base, the other to the top. It remains a mystery as to how safe this bridge is, so it would be best to stay off and view it from a distance.

DEVIL'S BRIDGE TRAIL

```
0        ½        1 MILE
```

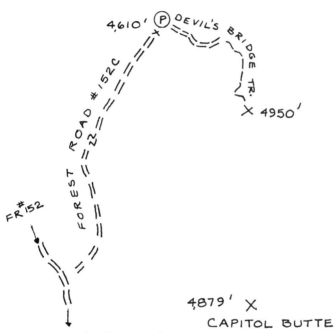

4,610' (P) DEVIL'S BRIDGE TR.

FOREST ROAD #152C

× 4950'

FR #152

DRY CREEK RD. TO 89A

4,879' × CAPITOL BUTTE

WINTER SPRING SUMMER FALL

	HARD SURFACE		SPRING
	LIGHT DUTY	⁀⁀	RIM
=====	UNIMPROVED	⌒	CORRAL
-----	TRAIL	×	PEAK
+++++	RAILROAD	Ⓟ	TRAILHEAD
■ ■	BUILDINGS	P.	PARKING
O	WATER TANK	⌂	WATER
Å	CAMPSITE	~	RIVER
×5270	ELEVATION CHECK	~...~.	DRAINAGE

WOODCHUTE TRAIL

ATTRACTION: A chance to hike under the actual location of a chute that carried logs to Jerome's smelters in its heyday; magnificent views

REQUIREMENTS: 5 hours one way; food, water, map

LOCATION: Woodchute Mountain, Jerome

DIFFICULTY: Moderate

ELEVATIONS: 5465'-7830'-7100'

LENGTH: 7 miles one way

MAPS REQUIRED: Hickey Mountain Quadrangle, 7.5 minute topographic, Yavapai County; Munds Draw Quadrangle, 7.5 minute topographic, Yavapai County

PERMIT : No

BIKES : No

EQUESTRIAN : Yes

WATER: Not dependable, bring your own

INFORMATION: Car shuttle is ideal from trail ends; hiking north to south is uphill

FIREARMS: Yes

PETS ON LEASH: Yes, on 6' leash only

TRAIL INFORMATION

To get to the trailhead, take Forest Road 318A west out of Jerome about 5 miles to a very visible parking area. This is the very upper end of the trail (starting point). South or lower end of trail is located about 3 miles southwest of Jerome near Forest Road 106. A right turn here and about one-half mile is a parking area and trail's end. Car shuttle required.

Trail climbs out of the upper parking area about 2400' on its way to the top of Woodchute Mountain. After you break out of the pines on top of Woodchute Mountain, spectacular views of Verde, Chino and Lonesome Valleys are to be seen. The remaining portion of trail is gentle as you descend to the campground near Forest Road #106 and trail's end. F.R. #106 is not an all-weather road.

WOODCHUTE TRAIL

1   0   1 MILE

WINTER SPRING SUMMER FALL

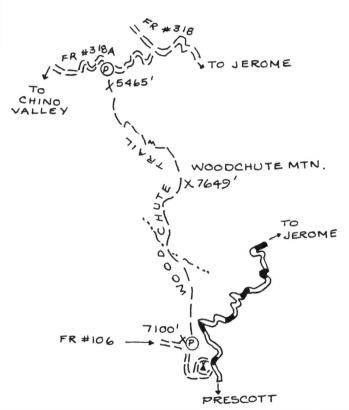

FR #318A

FR #318

TO JEROME

TO CHINO VALLEY

X 5465'

TRAIL

WOODCHUTE MTN.

X 7649'

WOODCHUTE

TO JEROME

FR #106 →

7100'

X ℗

PRESCOTT

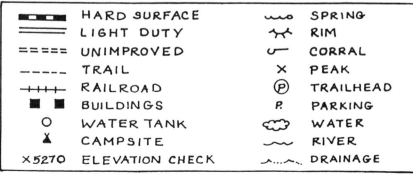

▰▱▰	HARD SURFACE	ᵔᵔᵒ	SPRING
═══	LIGHT DUTY	⋎⋏⋎	RIM
=====	UNIMPROVED	⌣	CORRAL
-----	TRAIL	×	PEAK
+++++	RAILROAD	℗	TRAILHEAD
■ ■	BUILDINGS	P.	PARKING
○	WATER TANK	☁	WATER
▲	CAMPSITE	∿	RIVER
×5270	ELEVATION CHECK	⌁....⌁	DRAINAGE

Stone ramada at Telegraph Pass on National Trail.

Chinese Wall on National Trail.

NATIONAL TRAIL

ATTRACTION: Views of complete Phoenix area as well as all points south; follows length of South Mountain

REQUIREMENTS: 6-8 hours hiking time one way; food, water, rain gear, maps

LOCATION: South Mountain Park, South Mountain, Phoenix

DIFFICULTY: Moderate to difficult

ELEVATIONS: 1320'-2360'-1575'

LENGTH: 12.5 miles plus 1 mile hike to parking lot at the end

MAPS REQUIRED: Laveen Quadrangle; Lone Butte Quadrangle; Guadalupe Quadrangle; 7.5 minute series topographic, Maricopa County

PERMIT: No, except for alcohol at picnics

BIKES: Yes, non-motorized

EQUESTRIAN: No

WATER: No

INFORMATION: Some rocky areas, very hot in summer, no camping, no glass containers

FIREARMS: No

PETS ON LEASH: Yes, on leash only

TRAIL INFORMATION

A car shuttle at both ends of trail works best. Enter the park from South Central Avenue from Phoenix; check in at guardhouse and proceed just over 4 miles to the San Juan parking area and trailhead. Correct trail skirts the road on which you just drove, as it skirts Maricopa Peak, crosses San Juan Road, drops into and crosses a wash, and then gets steep only long enough to ascend Goat Hill.

It is now a ridge trail. A left turn where the trail splits just before the ridge is correct. Continue east past the left turn for Ranger Trail to a stone ramada at Telegraph Pass, which is the halfway point. Trail now drops to and follows Summit Road for 150 yards, then switches back up for a bit and follows Summit Road for about one mile before reaching the TV towers. Trail again drops, crosses T.V.Road and proceeds to a natural wonder called Chinese Wall

NATIONAL TRAIL

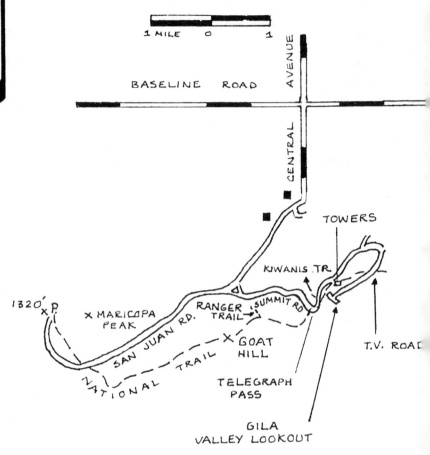

on the right. Once again trail crosses road into Buena Vista parking area and descends from east end of lot.

At next four-way intersection, continue straight; at next intersection for Hidden Valley continue straight also, and go straight again at the next intersection where Mormon Trail goes left. At one more intersection, where Hidden Valley goes to the right, is a 10-minute side trip to the right for Natural Arch and the tunnel, after which you return to National Trail.

Trail now descends faster and, as more cuts appear in the mountain, watch for 4 x 4 posts to guide you to the Pima Canyon

NATIONAL TRAIL

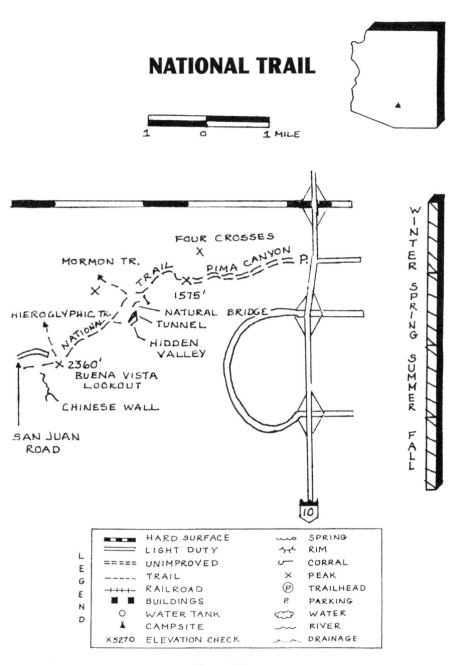

trailhead at the east end of South Mountain. It is now a 1-mile hike on gravel road (no cars) to Pima Canyon parking area and your other car. The Pima Canyon parking area is reached by car by taking Guadalupe Road west into South Mountain Park.

WIND CAVE TRAIL

ATTRACTION: A closeup view of the erosion pockets carved into the mountain, into the tuff layer laid down long ago

REQUIREMENTS: 1 hour one way; snack, water, map

LOCATION: Usery Mountain Regional Park, Apache Junction

DIFFICULTY: Moderate to difficult

ELEVATIONS: 2020'-2840'

LENGTH: 1.3 miles one way

MAPS REQUIRED: Apache Junction Quadrangle; 7.5 minute series topographic, Maricopa County; Usery Mountain Recreation Park Map

PERMIT: May be a day use fee in some areas; check with Park Ranger, it all depends on your activities.

BIKES: No

EQUESTRIAN: No

WATER: Bring your own

INFORMATION: Send for information on this park so that you are able to enjoy it to the fullest

FIREARMS: No

PETS ON LEASH: Yes, on 6' leash only

TRAIL INFORMATION

To reach the trailhead, take Usery Park Road north out of Apache Junction to Wind Cave Drive, and follow to picnic area #8 by the restrooms.

Trail leaves from here and, without the aid of a lot of switchbacks, climbs abruptly to the actual wind caves carved here over the years. There is not much shade to be had and it's very hot in summer. There are fine views of Apache Junction and seemingly endless views to the south.

The trail from the wind caves to the top isn't maintained, so it's best to return the way you came.

WIND CAVE TRAIL

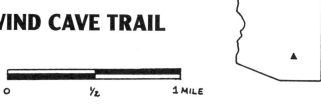

0   ½   1 MILE

USERY
MOUNTAIN
RECREATION
AREA

WIND CAVE TRAIL

X 2840'

TO USERY
PASS RD.   2020' X
            P

PICNIC
AREA

TONTO NATIONAL FOREST

WINTER SPRING SUMMER FALL

▬▬▬	HARD SURFACE	⌒o	SPRING
═══	LIGHT DUTY	⋏⋏⋏	RIM
═════	UNIMPROVED	⌐	CORRAL
-----	TRAIL	X	PEAK
┼┼┼┼	RAILROAD	Ⓟ	TRAILHEAD
■ ■	BUILDINGS	P.	PARKING
O	WATER TANK	☁	WATER
▲	CAMPSITE	⌒	RIVER
X5270	ELEVATION CHECK	⌒⋯⌒	DRAINAGE

RAINBOW VALLEY TRAIL

ATTRACTION: Longest trail in the park with many other connecting trail opportunities; a gem of a horseback ride; nice views

REQUIREMENTS: 7 hours round trip; food, water, rain gear, map

LOCATION: Estrella Mountain Regional Park, Goodyear

DIFFICULTY: Moderate to difficult - distance

ELEVATIONS: 900'-1460'-900'

LENGTH: 15.7 miles loop hike

MAPS REQUIRED: Avondale SE-SW Quadrangle, 7.5 minute topographic, Maricopa County
Tolleson Quadrangle, 7.5 minute topographic, Maricopa County
Perryville Quadrangle, 7.5 minute topographic, Maricopa County
Trail not on these maps but they allow you to study the area and terrain. The park map you will receive has trails transposed onto it.

PERMIT : May be a day use fee in some areas; check with Park Ranger; it all depends on your activities

BIKES : No

EQUESTRIAN : Yes

WATER: Best to bring your own

INFORMATION: Send for information on this park so you are able to enjoy it to the fullest

FIREARMS: No

PETS ON LEASH: Yes, 6' leash only

TRAIL INFORMATION

Trailhead is 18 miles southwest of Phoenix off State Route 85. Take Bullard Avenue south from S.R. 85 for two miles, cross the Gila River, then turn right on West Vineyard Avenue and travel one-quarter mile to Estrella Mountain Regional Park.

When you arrive, trail signs should be evident or else inquire at the Ranger Station. The trail you follow will be marked by the letter "A" on your park map.

Trail heads southwest as it starts to climb over a small hill,

RAINBOW VALLEY TRAIL

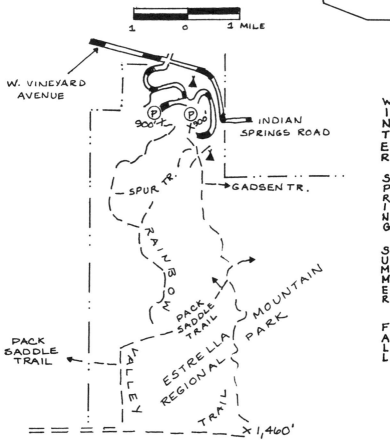

1   0   1 MILE

W. VINEYARD AVENUE

P   900'   P   x 900'

INDIAN SPRINGS ROAD

SPUR TR.

GADSEN TR.

RAINBOW

PACK SADDLE TRAIL

PACK SADDLE TRAIL

VALLEY

ESTRELLA MOUNTAIN REGIONAL PARK

TRAIL

X 1,460'

WINTER SPRING SUMMER FALL

▰▱▰	HARD SURFACE	ᵚᵒ	SPRING
═══	LIGHT DUTY	ʌʌ	RIM
=====	UNIMPROVED	ᵕ	CORRAL
-----	TRAIL	X	PEAK
┼┼┼┼	RAILROAD	Ⓟ	TRAILHEAD
■ ■	BUILDINGS	P.	PARKING
O	WATER TANK	☁	WATER
⚑	CAMPSITE	∿	RIVER
X 5270	ELEVATION CHECK	⌒⋯⌒	DRAINAGE

gaining a few hundred feet in altitude before again losing altitude as quickly as you gained it. Before entering a shallow canyon, Spur Trail is to the left, and shortly into the canyon the other leg of Spur Trail is encountered; continue straight both times. Shortly after leaving this canyon you will join the "Pack Saddle Historical Trail" via right turn for about one mile, before it again leaves and heads west; continue straight or south.

For about the next 5 miles over rather flat ground, the trail will loop and again head north as you skirt some rolling hills on your right. You will soon "T" into the Pack Saddle Historical Trail. Turn right on this trail and, in one-quarter mile, again travel north or left. Again you will enter a shallow canyon for a short distance on what is not only Rainbow Valley Trail, but Gadsden Trail as well. In about 2 miles you will cross Rock Knob Buggie Trail. In less than 1000' you will continue past Spur Trail trailhead for one-half mile to the start of your hike.

A familiar sight on many of Arizona's trails!

ARAVAIPA CANYON TRAIL

ATTRACTION: A chance to enjoy a true wilderness area along with a permanent flowing stream and a lot of wildlife; good photographic opportunities.

REQUIREMENTS: 10 to 12 hours one way; food, water, map

LOCATION: Aravaipa Canyon Wilderness Area. Southwest of Winkleman

DIFFICULTY: Moderate; 15" deep stream wading as well as some heavy brush areas

ELEVATIONS: 2630'-3060' west to east

LENGTH: 7 miles one way

REQUIREMENTS: Brandenberg Mountain Quadrangle, 7.5 minute topographic, Pinal County; Booger Canyon Quadrangle, 7.5 minute topographic, Graham County

PERMIT : Yes, call the Safford Ranger District at 602-428-4040

BIKES : No

EQUESTRIAN : Not over 5 horses per party, and horses are not allowed to remain in the canyon overnight

WATER: Although creek always flows, it is still best to carry your own

INFORMATION: Important information about this fragile area is too extensive for this book. Send to the B.L.M.-Safford Office for information and study it well to protect this area

FIREARMS: Some hunting is allowed and, again, a permit is required. Call the Safford Ranger District at 602-428-4040.

PETS ON LEASH: No

TRAIL INFORMATION

WEST TRAILHEAD: Access roads suitable for passenger cars yearlong.

From Phoenix (120 miles/2 to 2.5 hours): Take US Highway 60 to Superior. At Superior, take State Highway 177 to Winkleman. At Winkleman, take State Highway 77 11 miles to Aravaipa Road and travel 12 miles to the West trailhead—a paved and graded dirt

ARAVAIPA CANYON TRAIL

TRUE NORTH

1   0   1 MILE

WINTER SPRING SUMMER FALL

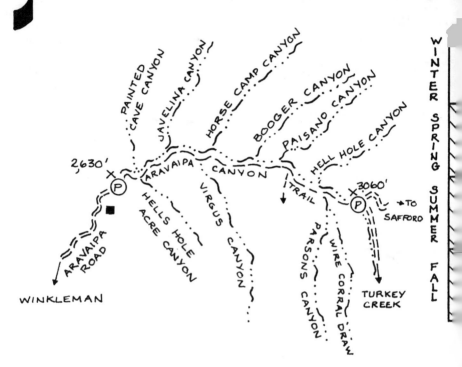

PAINTED CAVE CANYON

JAVELINA CANYON

HORSE CAMP CANYON

BOOGER CANYON

PAISANO CANYON

HELL HOLE CANYON

2,630' ×

(P)

ARAVAIPA CANYON TRAIL

3060' ×

(P)

→TO SAFFORD

HELLS ACRE CANYON

VIRGUS CANYON

ARAVAIPA ROAD

WINKLEMAN

PARSONS CANYON

WIRE CORRAL DRAW

TURKEY CREEK

LEGEND

▬▭▬	HARD SURFACE	‿o	SPRING
═══	LIGHT DUTY	⋎⋏	RIM
=====	UNIMPROVED	ᴗ	CORRAL
-----	TRAIL	×	PEAK
+++++	RAILROAD	(P)	TRAILHEAD
■ ■	BUILDINGS	P.	PARKING
O	WATER TANK	⌘	WATER
⚑	CAMPSITE	‿	RIVER
×5270	ELEVATION CHECK	ᴧ...ᴧ	DRAINAGE

road.

From Tucson (70 miles/1.5 to 2 hours): Take US Highway 89 to Oracle Junction. At Oracle Junction, take State Highway 77 to the Aravaipa Road, 8 miles north of Mammoth. Turn right on Aravaipa Road and travel 12 miles to the West trailhead—a paved and graded dirt road.

EAST TRAILHEAD Access roads suitable for passenger cars except for occasional washouts during July and August rains. Call ahead for conditions during this season.

From Phoenix (190 miles/4.5 to 5 hours): Take US Highway 60 from Phoenix to Globe. At Globe, continue on US Highway 70 to the Klondyke Road (8 miles east of Fort Thomas). Take this improved dirt road 45 miles to the East trailhead. Five stream crossings, suitable for passenger cars, will be encountered in the last 10 miles.

From Tucson (150 miles/2.5 to 3 hours): Take Interstate 10 east to Willcox. At Willcox, take exit 340, the graded dirt Ft. Grant Road north to Bonita. At Bonita, turn left and continue 40 miles to the East trailhead. Five stream crossings, suitable for passenger cars, will be encountered in the last 10 miles.

Enter canyon from the west. There is camping here overnight and, by doing so, you will get a fresh start on the trail in the morning. Old tennis shoes seem to work best because of the wading.

There is a trailhead sign for both ends at the trailhead and these are the last signs you will see the entire length of your hike. There is no real trail description as there is no real trail. It is a matter of staying in and following the main canyon. It requires wading back and forth across the stream and even hiking in the brush at times. You need to keep in mind that you are nearing the end of your hike after nine side canyons.

This is truly a hike like no other, as chances for wildlife and photography are endless. Be sure to send for more information for this hike and make sure you understand it.

BULL PASTURE TRAIL

ATTRACTION: When hiking up to Bull Pasture on Estes Canyon Trail, use Bull Pasture Trail down for a perfect round trip.

REQUIREMENTS: 1.2 hours hiking time one way; snack, water, map

LOCATION: Ajo Mountains, Pima County; Organ Pipe Cactus National Monument, Ajo

DIFFICULTY: Difficult

ELEVATIONS: 2440'-3200'

LENGTH: 1.8 miles one way

MAPS REQUIRED: Organ Pipe Cactus National Monument full park map, available at Visitor Center or Southwest Parks & Monuments, Phoenix

PERMIT: Yes (entrance fee is permit)

BIKES: No

EQUESTRIAN: No

WATER: No

INFORMATION: Proper topo map is outdated and does not show trails. Hike early in the day to avoid heat on this trail.

FIREARMS: No

PETS ON LEASH: No

TRAIL INFORMATION

Directly across from visitor center is the Ajo Mountain Drive (21 miles long). At mile 14.5 is the Estes Canyon picnic area and trailhead. In about 75 yards, the trail splits and Estes Canyon Trail starts to the left; continue on trail to the right. There are switchbacks for the next mile and it is rocky, but it is the shortest way up the mountain with nice views. At the 1-mile mark is the termination of Estes Canyon Trail; continue straight, again uphill.

In .5 mile you will arrive at Bull Pasture. This is an area surrounded by towering cliffs where farmers wintered cattle. Area is rocky.

You may consider taking Estes Canyon Trail back to the trailhead. Although longer, it is a nice round trip and more gentle.

BULL PASTURE TRAIL

0   ½   1 MILE

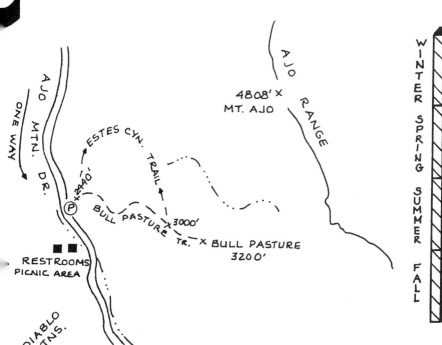

AJO MTN. DR.

ONE WAY

ESTES CYN. TRAIL

×2440'

Ⓟ

BULL PASTURE TR.

×3000'

× BULL PASTURE
3200'

4808' ×
MT. AJO

AJO RANGE

WINTER SPRING SUMMER FALL

■ ■
RESTROOMS
PICNIC AREA

DIABLO
MTNS.

▬▬▬	HARD SURFACE	ᗈᗯᗐ SPRING
═══	LIGHT DUTY	⋏⋏ RIM
═════	UNIMPROVED	ᴗ CORRAL
-----	TRAIL	× PEAK
+++++	RAILROAD	Ⓟ TRAILHEAD
■ ■	BUILDINGS	P. PARKING
○	WATER TANK	☁ WATER
▲	CAMPSITE	～ RIVER
×5270	ELEVATION CHECK	～…～ DRAINAGE

ESTES CANYON TRAIL

ATTRACTION: It's the easiest way to Bull Pasture, then use Bull Pasture Trail down for a perfect round trip.

REQUIREMENTS: 1 hour hiking time one way; snack, water, map

LOCATION: Ajo Mountains, Pima County; Organ Pipe Cactus National Monument, Ajo

DIFFICULTY: Moderate to difficult

ELEVATIONS: 2440'-3000'

LENGTH: 2.3 miles one way

MAPS REQUIRED: Organ Pipe Cactus National Monument full park map, available at Visitor Center or Southwest Parks & Monuments, Phoenix

PERMIT: Yes (entrance fee is permit)

BIKES: No

EQUESTRIAN: No

WATER: No

INFORMATION: Proper topo map is outdated and does not show trails. Hike early in the day to avoid heat on this trail.

FIREARMS: No

PETS ON LEASH: No

TRAIL INFORMATION

Directly across from Visitor Center is the Ajo Mountain Drive (21 miles long). At mile 14.5 is the Estes Canyon picnic area and trailhead. In about 75 yards, the trail splits and Bull Pasture Trail starts to the right; continue to the left. Trail is gentle through Estes Canyon as the scenery improves with every step; also, watch for wildlife.

At 1.5 miles, the trail climbs for the next .6 mile on rocky terrain (watch your step) and then dead ends at Bull Pasture Trail.

A left turn on Bull Pasture Trail, again uphill, will take you to Bull Pasture in .5 mile. This is an area surrounded by towering cliffs where farmers wintered cattle. Area is rocky!

From here, you may consider taking Bull Pasture Trail back to the trailhead. It makes a nice round trip and is shorter.

ESTES CANYON TRAIL

0   ½   1 MILE

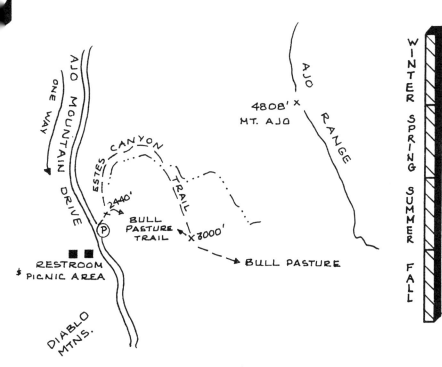

AJO MOUNTAIN DRIVE

ONE WAY

ESTES CANYON TRAIL

AJO RANGE

4808' X
MT. AJO

2440'
+

BULL
PASTURE
TRAIL

X 3000'

→ BULL PASTURE

P

RESTROOM
$ PICNIC AREA

DIABLO MTNS.

WINTER SPRING SUMMER FALL

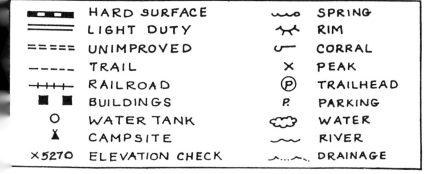

▬▭▬ HARD SURFACE	ᨓo	SPRING
═══ LIGHT DUTY	ᚷᚷ	RIM
===== UNIMPROVED	ᴗ	CORRAL
------ TRAIL	×	PEAK
+++++ RAILROAD	Ⓟ	TRAILHEAD
■ ■ BUILDINGS	P.	PARKING
O WATER TANK	☁	WATER
⚐ CAMPSITE	∿	RIVER
×5270 ELEVATION CHECK	∿…∿	DRAINAGE

VICTORIA MINE TRAIL

ATTRACTION: Easy rolling terrain; this hike allows a glimpse into the mining era 100 years ago; nice views

REQUIREMENTS: 1 hour hiking time one way; snack, water, map

LOCATION: Sonoita Mountains, Pima County; Organ Pipe Cactus National Monument, Ajo

DIFFICULTY: Easy

ELEVATIONS: 1680'-1640'

LENGTH: 2.25 miles one way

MAPS REQUIRED: Organ Pipe Cactus National Monument full park map, available at Visitor Center or Southwest Parks & Monuments, Phoenix

PERMIT: Yes (entrance fee is permit)

BIKES: No

EQUESTRIAN: No

WATER: NO

INFORMATION: Proper topo map is outdated and does not show trails. Use extreme caution around any old mines.

FIREARMS: No

PETS ON LEASH: No

TRAIL INFORMATION

From Visitor Center, take road to campground; at the guardhouse you are instructed where to park.

This is an easy hike over very gentle, rolling terrain. Trail is easy to follow with benches in some shady areas to escape the sun. Watch for unusual rocks along the trail. Mining evidence will come into view and, at .3 mile before the mine, the trail turns left onto an old 4-wheel-drive road to your destination.

The walls still stand from an old store and, of course, a lot of old mining ruins. All of this area is dangerous, especially off trail and on hillsides; use extreme caution.

Return the way you came.

VICTORIA MINE TRAIL

0   ½   1 MILE

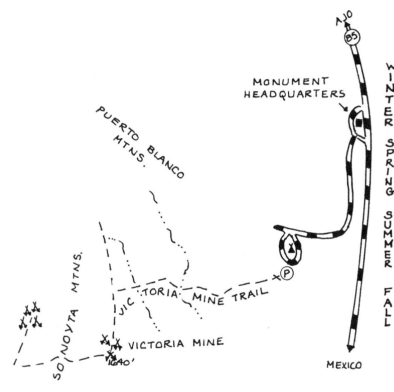

MONUMENT
HEADQUARTERS

PUERTO BLANCO MTNS.

SONOYTA MTNS.

VICTORIA MINE TRAIL

VICTORIA MINE
1640'

AJO

MEXICO

WINTER SPRING SUMMER FALL

▬▬▬	HARD SURFACE	∿∿⊙	SPRING
═══	LIGHT DUTY	⋎⋏⋎	RIM
≡≡≡≡≡	UNIMPROVED	⌒	CORRAL
‒‒‒‒‒	TRAIL	✕	PEAK
┼┼┼┼	RAILROAD	Ⓟ	TRAILHEAD
■ ■	BUILDINGS	P.	PARKING
○	WATER TANK	☁	WATER
▲	CAMPSITE	∿	RIVER
✕5270	ELEVATION CHECK	∿...∿	DRAINAGE

SABINO CANYON TRAIL

ATTRACTION: Fine views of several canyons; excellent camp-sites; many trail possibilities; study your map

REQUIREMENTS: 1.1 hours hiking time one way; food, water, rain gear, map

LOCATION: Santa Catalina Mountains, Tucson

DIFFICULTY: Easy

ELEVATIONS: 3325'-3720'

LENGTH: 2.5 miles one way

MAPS REQUIRED: Santa Catalina Mountain Trail and Recreation map, basic 15 minute series, U.S. Forest Service

PERMIT: No

BIKES: No

EQUESTRIAN: Moderate to easy

WATER: Yes, purify

INFORMATION: Must either use Sabino Canyon-Phone Line Trail or tram to reach this trailhead

FIREARMS: Yes

PETS ON LEASH: Yes

TRAIL INFORMATION

Access to this trailhead can be reached two ways, either by taking the tram from Sabino Canyon Visitor Center to the end of the road in Upper Sabino Canyon, or by hiking less than a mile to Lower Sabino Canyon recreation area from the Visitor Center. Here is the trailhead to Phone Line Trail that travels up the canyon 4.7 miles to the Sabino Canyon trailhead.

From the upper road, the trail makes switchbacks from the start for about .5 mile before turning left heading northeast up Sabino Canyon.

Traveling well above the canyon bottom, one can visualize the dam that was almost built here long ago. Trail continues above the creek to its end, where it drops into Sabino Basin.

At this intersection, Hutch's Pool is to your left (an excellent way to continue to the high country) and Bear Canyon is to the right. A bit of planning provides other possibilities as well.

SABINO CANYON TRAIL

0   ½   1 MILE

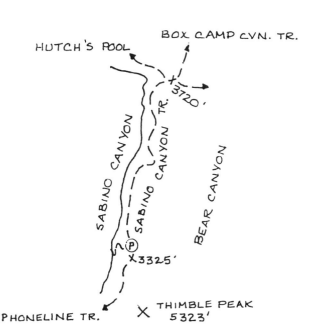

HUTCH'S POOL

BOX CAMP CVN. TR.

3720'

SABINO CANYON

SABINO CANYON TR.

BEAR CANYON

(P) X 3325'

PHONELINE TR.

THIMBLE PEAK
5323'

WINTER SPRING SUMMER FALL

TRUE NORTH

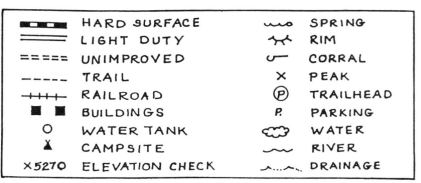

▬▬▬	HARD SURFACE		◡◦	SPRING
═══	LIGHT DUTY		⋏⋏	RIM
═════	UNIMPROVED		◡	CORRAL
-----	TRAIL		×	PEAK
┼┼┼┼	RAILROAD		Ⓟ	TRAILHEAD
■ ■	BUILDINGS		P.	PARKING
○	WATER TANK		⌒⌒⌒	WATER
▲	CAMPSITE		~~~	RIVER
×5270	ELEVATION CHECK		⌒...⌒	DRAINAGE

MOUNT LEMMON TRAIL

ATTRACTION: Hutch's Pool and on to the third highest peak in southern Arizona; fantastic panorama

REQUIREMENTS: 4 hours hiking time one way; food, water, rain gear, map

LOCATION: Santa Catalina Mountains, Tucson

DIFFICULTY: Moderate to difficult

ELEVATIONS: 7500'-9010'

LENGTH: 5.8 miles one way

MAPS REQUIRED: Santa Catalina Mountain Trail and Recreation map, basic 15 minute series, U.S. Forest Service

PERMIT: No

BIKES: No

EQUESTRIAN: Moderate to difficult

WATER: Yes, purify; should bring own

INFORMATION: This trail not for a novice; do not attempt this trail unless in excellent condition; be well supplied

FIREARMS: Yes

PETS ON LEASH: Yes

TRAIL INFORMATION

Trail head is located at the intersection of Romero Canyon Trail and West Fork Trail west of Sabino Basin. It is a true introduction to the high country.

At this point, you are just over half way to the top. A left turn would eventually drop you into Catalina State Park; continue to the right. Trail climbs moderately via a few switchbacks for the next 1.9 miles. Views over you shoulder here are almost second to none. Soon you arrive at the next intersection and the Wilderness of Rocks Trail to the right with all of its creations; continue to the left. Still climbing, the next 2.4 miles take you to the Cañada Del Oro Trail intersection and an old road. Sutherland, Samaniego Ridge and Cañada Del Oro Trails are to your left. Continue to the right on a service road past Lemmon Park Trail and Lemmon Rock Trail. Remain on road to summit, the highest point in the Catalinas. (It works well to have a car here or to have arranged to be picked up.)

MOUNT LEMMON TRAIL

TRUE NORTH

1   0   1 MILE

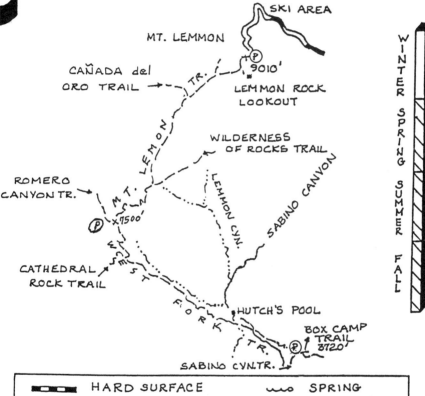

SKI AREA

MT. LEMMON

CAÑADA del
ORO TRAIL →

TR.

P
9010'

LEMMON ROCK
LOOKOUT

WILDERNESS
OF ROCKS TRAIL

MT. LEMMON

LEMMON CYN.

SABINO CANYON

ROMERO
CANYON TR. →

P   X 7500

WEST

CATHEDRAL
ROCK TRAIL →

FORK

HUTCH'S POOL

BOX CAMP
TRAIL
3720'

TR.

P

SABINO CYN. TR.

WINTER SPRING SUMMER FALL

▬▬▬	HARD SURFACE	∿o	SPRING
═══	LIGHT DUTY	⅄	RIM
=====	UNIMPROVED	⌣	CORRAL
-----	TRAIL	X	PEAK
++++	RAILROAD	℗	TRAILHEAD
■ ■	BUILDINGS	P.	PARKING
O	WATER TANK	☁	WATER
▲	CAMPSITE	∿	RIVER
X 5270	ELEVATION CHECK	∿...∿	DRAINAGE

PIMA CANYON TRAIL

ATTRACTION: Travels up Pima Canyon to the summit of Mt. Kimball. Fantastic views.

REQUIREMENTS: 4 hours hiking time one way; food, water, rain gear, map

LOCATION: Santa Catalina Mountains, Tucson

DIFFICULTY: Easy then difficult

ELEVATIONS: 2950'-7255'

LENGTH: 7.1 miles one way

MAPS REQUIRED: Santa Catalina Mountain Trail and Recreation map, basic 15 minute series, U.S. Forest Service

PERMIT: No

BIKES: No

EQUESTRIAN: No

WATER: Not dependable

INFORMATION: Area before trailhead on private property; access could be denied at any time; check at Visitor Center

FIREARMS: Yes

PETS ON LEASH: Only on first 3.2 miles

TRAIL INFORMATION

Trailhead is located at the end of Magee Road, just east of Oracle Road and is on private property, but can be used. Work is currently being done on a new trailhead.

Trail starts out very easy, except for staying on the right path. Do not follow canyon bottom but rather stay to the left higher up as your map indicates.

Soon you will enter the Coronado National Forest (it's marked). Trail climbs gently before dropping into, and now following, the canyon bottom for about 3 miles. These three miles are difficult as it slowly gets steeper, and because of a lot of overgrowth. After passing the second dam, it gets even steeper as it takes you to Pima Spring at about the 5-mile mark. Great rest or overnight area.

Trail climbs more aggressively now and wanders back and forth, but still follows the canyon to a fork where a left turn leads to a dead end, so make a right turn. It is a steep climb through often overgrown areas to Mt. Kimball at the trail's end. Views are superb.

PIMA CANYON TRAIL

1   0   1 MILE

W I N T E R   S P R I N G   S U M M E R   F A L L

PUSCH RIDGE

PIMA SPRING

PUSCH PEAK
5361' X

MT. KIMBALL
7255'
X

PIMA CANYON TRAIL

2950'

KIMBALL TRAIL

PIMA CANYON TRAIL

MAGEE RD.
(P) X

X 4385'
ROSEWOOD
POINT

HARD SURFACE	ᗢᵒ	**SPRING**
LIGHT DUTY	⅄⅄⅄	**RIM**
===== **UNIMPROVED**	ᶸ	**CORRAL**
----- **TRAIL**	×	**PEAK**
+++ **RAILROAD**	Ⓟ	**TRAILHEAD**
▪ ▪ **BUILDINGS**	P.	**PARKING**
○ **WATER TANK**	☁☁	**WATER**
▲ **CAMPSITE**	∿	**RIVER**
×5270 **ELEVATION CHECK**	∿...∿	**DRAINAGE**

GREEN MOUNTAIN TRAIL

ATTRACTION: Maverick Spring is well worth the .4 mile side trip; very nice area; nice views

REQUIREMENTS: 2 hours hiking time one way; food, water, rain gear, map

LOCATION: Santa Catalina Mountains, Tucson

DIFFICULTY: Moderate

ELEVATIONS: 7280'-6960'-6400'

LENGTH: 3.9 miles one way

MAPS REQUIRED: Santa Catalina Mountain Trail and Recreation map, basic 15 minute series, U.S. Forest Service

PERMIT: No

BIKES: Yes

EQUESTRIAN: Moderate

WATER: Yes, at Maverick Spring

INFORMATION: Nice car shuttle, San Pedro Vista on Mt. Lemmon Highway to General Hitchcock picnic area

FIREARMS: Yes

PETS ON LEASH: Yes

TRAIL INFORMATION

High above Tucson on the Mt. Lemmon Highway is the San Pedro Vista and the trailhead as well—park here.

Trail starts to climb ever so gently for just 1/4 mile to your encounter with your first intersection, where a left turn would connect you with Brush Corral Trail, so continue straight. Trail now follows a ridge before descending. Another seldom-used trail is encountered where a left turn also connects you with Brush Canyon Trail; again continue straight.

In just under .5 mile, a left turn takes you on an interesting side trip to Maverick Spring. This .4 mile one-way trail to the spring takes you to an area almost too nice to leave.

Backtrack to main trail and continue as the trail climbs to Bear Saddle, where a left turn would take you to Guthrie Mountain. Continue straight as trail starts descending as you near Horse Camp Spring. After crossing the creek several times, you arrive at General Hitchcock picnic ground. A car pool works well for this hike.

GREEN MOUNTAIN TRAIL

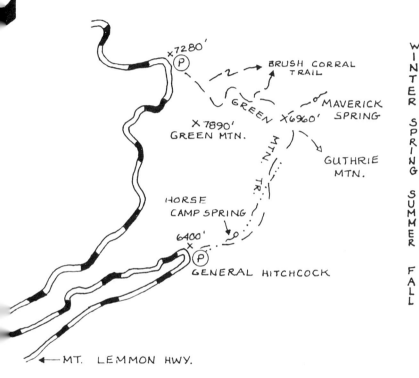

WILDERNESS OF ROCKS TRAIL

ATTRACTION: Very interesting geological area—one of the best in the Catalinas; nice picnicking; nice views

REQUIREMENTS: 2.0 hours hiking time one way; food, water, rain gear, map

LOCATION: Santa Catalina Mountains, Tucson

DIFFICULTY: Moderate

ELEVATIONS: 7280'-8000'

LENGTH: 4.0 miles one way

MAPS REQUIRED: Santa Catalina Mountain Trail and Recreation map, basic 15 minute series, U.S. Forest Service

PERMIT: No

BIKES: No

EQUESTRIAN: Moderate to difficult

WATER: Along Lemmon Creek

INFORMATION: Consult your maps for endless possibilities combining this trail with others; hard to follow in some areas

FIREARMS: Yes

PETS ON LEASH: No

TRAIL INFORMATION

By taking Marshall Trail for 1.2 miles along Lemon Creek from Marshall Gulch picnic area you will arrive at Marshall Saddle and the start of Wilderness of Rocks Trail. A lot of shade is to be enjoyed along this section until you reach the saddle, from which point Aspen Trail goes to the left and Radio Ridge to the right; continue straight. Having your climbing over now, you gradually lose altitude as the trail makes its way through a real "wilderness of rocks".

At about the 2.0 mile mark, high above you can be seen Lemmon Rock Lookout. The right turn at this intersection is a 2-mile trail that switchbacks to the lookout. This is a tough trail; do not consider it if not in shape.

Trail continues southwest crossing Lemmon Creek two more times and, as the trail gets a little harder to follow, you will find yourself alongside more formations than you can count.

Just before trail's end at the intersection of Mt. Lemmon Trail, you will encounter a slight climb to complete your hike. You can build your own hike from here.

WILDERNESS OF ROCKS TRAIL

o   ½   1 MILE

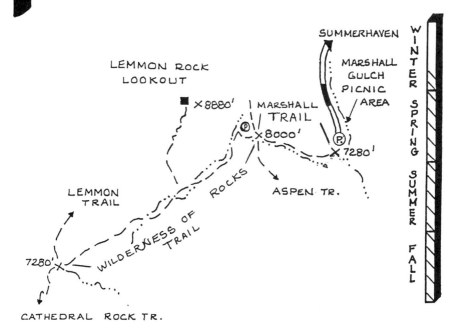

SUMMERHAVEN

MARSHALL GULCH PICNIC AREA

LEMMON ROCK LOOKOUT

×8880'   MARSHALL TRAIL

ⓟ   ×8000'

ⓟ   ×7280'

LEMMON TRAIL

WILDERNESS OF ROCKS TRAIL

ASPEN TR.

7280'×

CATHEDRAL ROCK TR.

WINTER SPRING SUMMER FALL

LEGEND

▬▭▬	HARD SURFACE	∽o	SPRING	
═══	LIGHT DUTY	⋏⋏⋏	RIM	
=====	UNIMPROVED	ᒕ	CORRAL	
-----	TRAIL	×	PEAK	
+++++	RAILROAD	ⓟ	TRAILHEAD	
▪ ▪	BUILDINGS	P	PARKING	
O	WATER TANK	⟅⟆	WATER	
⯭	CAMPSITE	∿	RIVER	
×5270	ELEVATION CHECK	∿…∿	DRAINAGE	

to 70%

SUNSET TRAIL

ATTRACTION: At Sunset Rock along trail is an excellent view down Sabino Canyon

REQUIREMENTS: 3/4 hour hiking time one way; food, water, rain gear, map

LOCATION: Santa Catalina Mountains, Tucson

DIFFICULTY: Easy

ELEVATIONS: 7440'-7725'

LENGTH: 1.6 miles one way

MAPS REQUIRED: Santa Catalina Mountain Trail and Recreation map; basic 15 minute series, U.S. Forest Service

PERMIT: No

BIKES: Yes

EQUESTRIAN: Easy

WATER: Not dependable

INFORMATION: At trail's end and only a very short distance by road is Mt. Lemmon Highway and also Butterfly Trail.

FIREARMS: Yes

PETS ON LEASH: Yes

TRAIL INFORMATION

High above Tucson on the Mt. Lemmon Highway you will come to a fork in the road leading to Ski Valley on the right, and through the tiny village of Summerhaven to the left; take the left fork. In about a mile, you will arrive at Marshall Gulch picnic area; park here.

Trail starts downhill on the north side of the creek and, after crossing another creek, the trail heads southeast. After climbing for only a short distance, it starts its horseshoe effect, staying almost level. Soon a faint route will take off to the creek; do not take this as it only travels to a gauging station.

Continue straight and, after about 3/4 mile and close to Bear Wallow Creek, you will see what is called Sunset Rock, as well as awesome views towards Sabino Canyon. Trail is easy now as a summer home area is reached and the end of the trail.

A road can now be hiked (very short) to Mt. Lemmon Highway. Butterfly Trail is almost directly across the highway.

SUNSET TRAIL

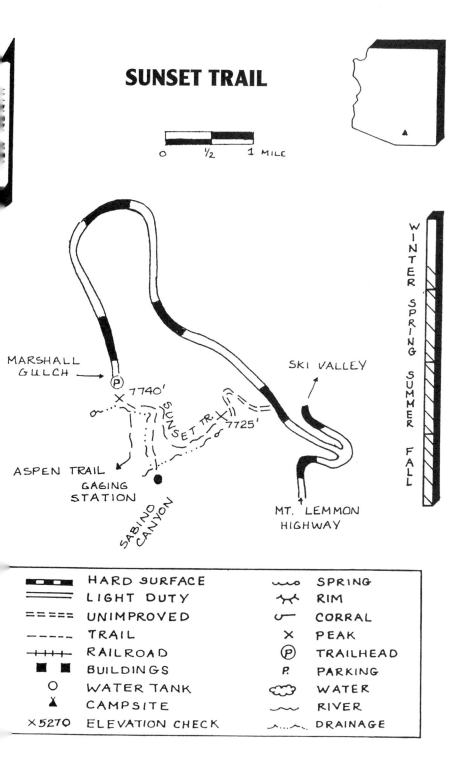

0   ½   1 MILE

MARSHALL GULCH

SKI VALLEY

7740'

SUNSET TR.

7725'

ASPEN TRAIL

GAGING STATION

SABINO CANYON

MT. LEMMON HIGHWAY

WINTER SPRING SUMMER FALL

	HARD SURFACE		SPRING
	LIGHT DUTY	⌁	RIM
=====	UNIMPROVED		CORRAL
-----	TRAIL	×	PEAK
+++++	RAILROAD	Ⓟ	TRAILHEAD
■ ■	BUILDINGS	P.	PARKING
O	WATER TANK		WATER
▲	CAMPSITE		RIVER
×5270	ELEVATION CHECK		DRAINAGE

PALISADE TRAIL

ATTRACTION: Views of entire Sabino Canyon; good camping area at Mud Spring

REQUIREMENTS: 4 hours hiking time one way; food, water, rain gear, map

LOCATION: Santa Catalina Mountains, Tucson

DIFFICULTY: Moderate to difficult

ELEVATIONS: 4080'-7850'

LENGTH: 6.8 miles one way

MAPS REQUIRED: Santa Catalina Mountain Trail and Recreation map; basic 15 minute series, U.S. Forest Service

PERMIT: No

BIKES: NO

EQUESTRIAN: Moderate to difficult

WATER: Just over halfway at Mud Spring; purify

INFORMATION: Good trail; some hard uphill so be prepared; very popular trail into the high country; altitudes vary

FIREARMS: Yes

PETS ON LEASH: Yes

TRAIL INFORMATION

For trailhead, travel east from Sabino Basin on Bear Canyon Trail, just over 1 mile to the left turn for Palisade Trail. Be prepared for switchbacks as several will be encountered on this trail. There are, however, flat areas as well where you can rest and enjoy fantastic views down Sabino Canyon. Also check out the geology on this trail.

For about the next mile, the trail heads into, and follows, Pine Canyon drainage to a popular overnight area at Mud Spring, at about the 5-mile mark.

The trail climbs moderately for the next 2 miles. Shortly after this, the trail levels just before the intersection to the Girl Scout camp. It's best to respect their privacy and bear left, continuing on to Showers Point Campground. Cars may be parked here or just over .5 mile at Palisade Ranger Station. It works well to arrange to be picked up at either of these two areas.

PALISADE TRAIL

1   0   1 MILE

TRUE NORTH

WINTER SPRING SUMMER FALL

SHOWERS POINT →
X 7850'
GIRL SCOUT CAMP
PALISADE CANYON
PALISADE TRAIL
PINE CANYON
MUD SPRING
MOUNT LEMMON HWY.
ROSE PEAK X 7299'
SABINO CYN. TR.
Ⓟ X 4080'
BEAR CANYON TRAIL

	HARD SURFACE		SPRING
	LIGHT DUTY	⋏	RIM
=====	UNIMPROVED	⌒	CORRAL
-----	TRAIL	X	PEAK
++++	RAILROAD	Ⓟ	TRAILHEAD
■ ■	BUILDINGS	P.	PARKING
O	WATER TANK	☁	WATER
▲	CAMPSITE	∿	RIVER
X5270	ELEVATION CHECK	∿⋯∿	DRAINAGE

PONTATOC RIDGE TRAIL

ATTRACTION: Old mine at end of trail; nice day hike; scenery

REQUIREMENTS: 1.3 hours hiking time one way; food, water, rain gear, map

LOCATION: Santa Catalina Mountains, Tucson

DIFFICULTY: Moderate to difficult

ELEVATIONS: 3360'-5040'

LENGTH: 1.8 miles one way

MAPS REQUIRED: Santa Catalina Mountains Trail and Recreation map, basic 15 minute series, U.S. Forest Service

PERMIT: No

BIKES: No

EQUESTRIAN: Not recommended

WATER: Only when creek runs

INFORMATION: Take extreme care towards end of trail due to loose rocks above 100-foot dropoffs—hikers have died here; bad air in mine

FIREARMS: Yes

PETS ON LEASH: First 1.8 miles, prohibited from that point on

TRAIL INFORMATION

Pontatoc Canyon trailhead is at the north end of Alvernon Road in north Tucson. You must hike .8 mile on Pontatoc Canyon Trail before the Pontatoc Ridge Trail intersection is encountered.

First part of trail is a 4-wheel-drive road (no longer used). In about 1/3 mile, the true Pontatoc trail takes off to the right. During the next .5 mile, the trail drops into the wash but comes right back out and transverses several switchbacks to the Pontatoc Ridge trailhead.

After a very sharp right turn on the ridge trail, you will be traveling southwest, seemingly back where you came from. However, in no time at all, you will be traveling northeast and uphill, after making a sharp left turn on the main ridge trail. The reason for all this is that the original trailhead is blocked now by private property.

After Pontatoc saddle, the climb is harder and, as you approach the mine at trail's end, it is extremely unsafe to leave the trail due to very loose footing above high cliffs. Conditions in the mine are unsafe as well. *Be careful* and return the way you came.

PONTATOC RIDGE TRAIL

0 ½ 1 MILE

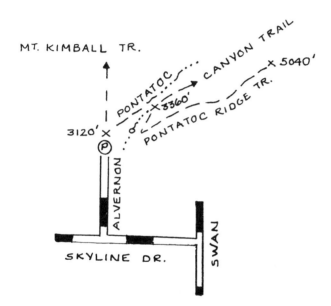

MT. KIMBALL TR.

PONTATOC CANYON TRAIL

X 5040'

X 3360'

PONTATOC RIDGE TR.

3120' X

Ⓟ

ALVERNON

SWAN

SKYLINE DR.

WINTER SPRING SUMMER FALL

HARD SURFACE	SPRING
LIGHT DUTY	RIM
UNIMPROVED	CORRAL
TRAIL	PEAK
RAILROAD	Ⓟ TRAILHEAD
BUILDINGS	P. PARKING
O WATER TANK	WATER
▲ CAMPSITE	RIVER
X5270 ELEVATION CHECK	DRAINAGE

PONTATOC CANYON TRAIL

ATTRACTION: Breathtaking views of high cliffs that form Pontatoc Ridge

REQUIREMENTS: 2.1 hours hiking time one way; food, water, rain gear, map

LOCATION: Santa Catalina Mountains, Tucson

DIFFICULTY: Moderate to difficult

ELEVATIONS: 3120'-5920'

LENGTH: 3.9 miles one way

MAPS REQUIRED: Santa Catalina Mountain Trail and Recreation map, basic 15 minute series, U.S. Forest Service

PERMIT: No

BIKES: No

EQUESTRIAN: Not recommended

WATER: Only when creek runs

INFORMATION: Trail past 3.9 mile mark is not for a novice as one can get lost here; it is best to turn around

FIREARMS: Yes

PETS ON LEASH: Allowed on first 3.9 miles only

TRAIL INFORMATION

The Pontatoc Canyon trailhead is at the north end of Alvernon Road in north Tucson.

First part of trail is a 4-wheel-drive road (no longer used). In about 1/3 mile, the true Pontatoc Canyon Trail takes off to the right. During the next .5 mile, the trail drops into the wash but comes right back out and transverses several switchbacks to the Pontatoc Ridge trailhead. Continue straight for Pontatoc Canyon Trail.

After a bit of a climb (rather minor), an intersection is encountered with an almost nonexistent trail to the right. Continue straight, climbing a bit more, before dropping into and crossing a creek. This is a nice area to rest and snack.

After climbing again for about 1/4 mile, another intersection is encountered where a right turn continues to the creek bottom; continue straight at the intersection for the Canyon Trail. After again climbing for almost another mile, the trail drops into the canyon, which is a good turnaround point. The trail does go on, climbs out of the canyon, then all but disappears, so it's rather pointless to try to go on. Return the way you came.

PONTATOC CANYON TRAIL

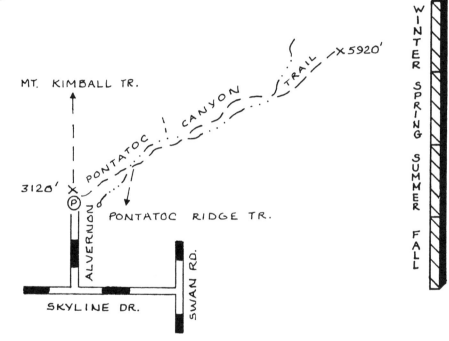

TRUE NORTH

0   ½   1 MILE

WINTER SPRING SUMMER FALL

MT. KIMBALL TR.

X 5920'

PONTATOC CANYON TRAIL

3120' X

Ⓟ

PONTATOC RIDGE TR.

ALVERNON

SWAN RD.

SKYLINE DR.

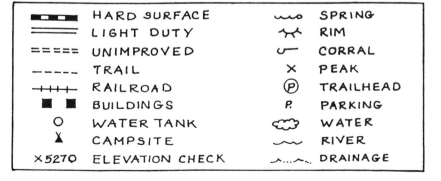

▭▬▭	HARD SURFACE	ᴗᴗo	SPRING
═══	LIGHT DUTY	⋏⋏⋏	RIM
═════	UNIMPROVED	ᴗ	CORRAL
-----	TRAIL	X	PEAK
++++	RAILROAD	Ⓟ	TRAILHEAD
■ ■	BUILDINGS	P.	PARKING
O	WATER TANK	☁	WATER
⋏	CAMPSITE	～～	RIVER
X5270	ELEVATION CHECK	⌒…⌒	DRAINAGE

MINT SPRING TRAIL

ATTRACTION: Nice camping area at Mint Spring

REQUIREMENTS: 3/4 hour hiking time one way; food, water, rain gear, map

LOCATION: Santa Catalina Mountains, Tucson

DIFFICULTY: Easy

ELEVATIONS: 8000'-8400'-8000'

LENGTH: 1.7 miles one way

MAPS REQUIRED: Santa Catalina Mountain Trail and Recreation map, basic 15 minute series, U.S. Forest Service

PERMIT: No

BIKES: No

EQUESTRIAN: Easy

WATER: Not dependable; purify

INFORMATION: Can be used as loop trail for many side trips. Study your map.

FIREARMS: Yes

PETS ON LEASH: No

TRAIL INFORMATION

High above Tucson on the Mt. Lemmon Highway, you will come to a fork in the road leading to Ski Valley on the right and to the tiny village of Summerhaven to the left; take the left fork.

In about .2 mile, you will encounter a turn to the right to Carter Canyon. Take this road to the end and find trailhead just past last dwelling and through a gate. Carter Canyon trailhead is close also, very noticeable.

As you can tell from your map, you will climb a bit for first part of trail (nothing severe) before coming to a delightful area at Mint Spring at about the halfway point. Perfect picnic conditions are present here among all the mint.

For the remaining .9 mile of trail, it stays almost level until you again lose all the altitude you had gained by the time you reach trail's end at Marshall Saddle.

At this point, four trails converge; it's fun to build your own hike from here.

MINT SPRING TRAIL

0   ½   1 MILE

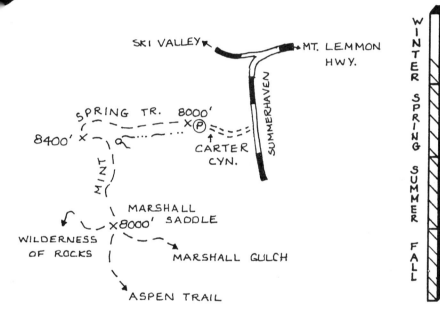

SKI VALLEY

MT. LEMMON HWY.

SUMMERHAVEN

SPRING TR. 8000'

8400' X

CARTER CYN.

MARSHALL SADDLE

X 8000'

WILDERNESS OF ROCKS

MARSHALL GULCH

ASPEN TRAIL

WINTER SPRING SUMMER FALL

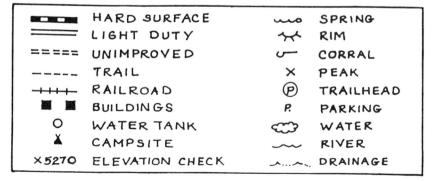

▰▰▰	HARD SURFACE	ᜑᜑo	SPRING
═══	LIGHT DUTY	⋌⋋	RIM
=====	UNIMPROVED	ᴗ	CORRAL
-----	TRAIL	X	PEAK
+++++	RAILROAD	Ⓟ	TRAILHEAD
■ ■	BUILDINGS	P.	PARKING
O	WATER TANK	ᙚ	WATER
▲	CAMPSITE	∿	RIVER
X 5270	ELEVATION CHECK	ᜑ...∿.	DRAINAGE

ASPEN TRAIL

ATTRACTION: Travels through a huge stand of aspens

REQUIREMENTS: 2 hour hiking time one way; food, water, rain gear, map

LOCATION: Santa Catalina Mountains, Tucson

DIFFICULTY: Moderate to difficult

ELEVATIONS: 7450'-9020'

LENGTH: 4.1 miles one way

MAPS REQUIRED: Santa Catalina Mountain Trail and Recreation map, basic 15 minute series, U.S. Forest Service

PERMIT : No

BIKES : No

EQUESTRIAN : Moderate to difficult

WATER: No

INFORMATION: By using other Trails along with Aspen, one can hike to ski lift. Study your map.

FIREARMS: Yes

PETS ON LEASH: No

TRAIL INFORMATION

High above Tucson on the Mt. Lemmon Highway, you will come to a fork in the road leading to Ski Valley on the right, and through the tiny village of Summerhaven to the left; take the left fork.

In another mile, you will arrive at Marshall Gulch picnic area. The trailhead is marked by a sign in the campground.

About 300' into the trail, you will see a fork; travel to the right uphill. After one-half mile, you will encounter switchbacks firmly placed in a mighty aspen grove. At about 1.5 miles, the switchbacks give way to level ground and another fork is encountered. A turn to the left takes you to Lunch Ledge, but you should travel to the right to Marshall Saddle at 8000'.

At this point, four trails converge. Marshall Gulch Campground is to the right and Wilderness of Rocks trail to the left. Trail continues straight ahead at the Saddle and grows a bit dim as switchbacks are encountered.

In only a short time good trail again appears and you will arrive at the upper end of the ski lift at Aspen Draw Trail.

ASPEN TRAIL

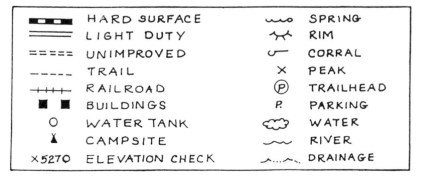

TRUE NORTH

0   ½   1 MILE

SKI LIFT

ASPEN TRAIL

X 9020'

SUMMERHAVEN

MARSHAL SADDLE
X 8000'

WILDERNESS OF ROCKS TR.

ASPEN TRAIL

P
X 7450'

MT. LEMMON HWY.

WINTER SPRING SUMMER FALL

	HARD SURFACE	⌣⌣o	SPRING
	LIGHT DUTY	✕✕✕	RIM
=====	UNIMPROVED	⌣	CORRAL
-----	TRAIL	✕	PEAK
+++++	RAILROAD	Ⓟ	TRAILHEAD
■ ■	BUILDINGS	P.	PARKING
O	WATER TANK	☁	WATER
▲	CAMPSITE	∿	RIVER
✕5270	ELEVATION CHECK	∿...∿	DRAINAGE

ESPERERO CANYON TRAIL

ATTRACTION: Most popular trail used to Cathedral Rock and the "Window" and on to the high country

REQUIREMENTS: 4.5 hours hiking time one way; food, water, rain gear, map

LOCATION: Santa Catalina Mountains, Tucson

DIFFICULTY: Moderate

ELEVATIONS: 2850'-7000'

LENGTH: 8.5 miles one way

MAPS REQUIRED: Santa Catalina Mountain Trail and Recreation map, basic 15 minute series, U.S. Forest Service

PERMIT : No

BIKES : No

EQUESTRIAN : Not recommended

WATER: Only when creek is running

INFORMATION: There is a 100' dropoff at the Window; use extreme caution

FIREARMS: Yes

PETS ON LEASH: No

TRAIL INFORMATION

Trailhead is reached by walking or taking tram from Sabino Canyon Visitor Center to the Cactus Picnic Area on Sabino Canyon Road (now closed to cars). The trail leaves the picnic area and transverses Rattlesnake Canyon, climbs a bit to a flat area, then descends again into the canyon. Please refer to your map to take note of the part of this trail that is on private land.

After crossing the canyon and starting to climb, it gets steep enough for switchbacks. After these, two saddles will be encountered before descending into Esperero Canyon at almost the halfway point on the trail.

Hiking now in the Esperero Canyon (uphill), the trail passes Norman Spring to Bridal Veil Falls at the 5.5 mile mark. Locate falls on your left (usually dry). It is now a climb of just under a mile to the intersection. A right turn takes you to Sabino Canyon and many choices from there (check map).

Esperero continues left, and climbs, at times by switchbacks, before descending to the Window at trail's end. Use caution.

ESPERERO CANYON TRAIL

1   0   1 MILE

TRUE NORTH

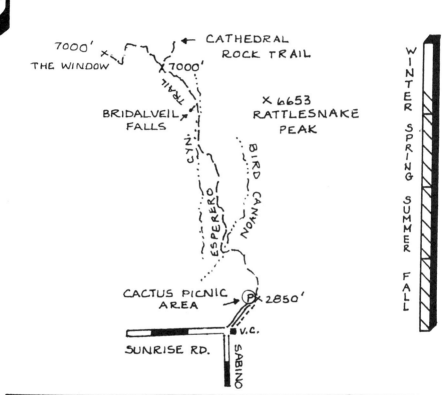

WINTER SPRING SUMMER FALL

CATHEDRAL ROCK TRAIL

7000'
THE WINDOW
7000'

BRIDALVEIL FALLS

X 6653 RATTLESNAKE PEAK

BIRD CANYON

CYN.

ESPERERO

CACTUS PICNIC AREA
P X 2850'

V.C.

SUNRISE RD.

SABINO

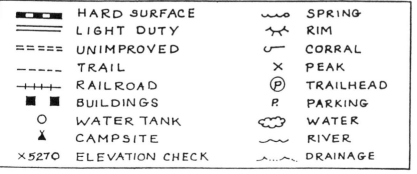

▄▄▄	HARD SURFACE	∿o	SPRING
═══	LIGHT DUTY	⋀⋀	RIM
═════	UNIMPROVED	⌒	CORRAL
-----	TRAIL	X	PEAK
++++	RAILROAD	Ⓟ	TRAILHEAD
▪ ▪	BUILDINGS	P.	PARKING
O	WATER TANK	☁	WATER
▲	CAMPSITE	∿	RIVER
X5270	ELEVATION CHECK	∿...∿	DRAINAGE

FINGER ROCK TRAIL

ATTRACTION: Travels to the summit of Mt. Kimball; excellent views

REQUIREMENTS: 3.5 hours hiking time one way; food, water, rain gear, map

LOCATION: Santa Catalina Mountains, Tucson

DIFFICULTY: Easy then difficult

ELEVATIONS: 3050'-7255'

LENGTH: 5 miles one way

MAPS REQUIRED: Santa Catalina Mountain Trail and Recreation map, basic 15 minute series, U.S. Forest Service

PERMIT : No

BIKES : No

EQUESTRIAN : Not recommended

WATER: Not dependable

INFORMATION: Author Harold Bell Wright is said to have camped along this trail; trail is rocky

FIREARMS: Yes

PETS ON LEASH: Only on first 1.1 miles of trail; prohibited from that point on

TRAIL INFORMATION

Trailhead is reached by traveling to the north end of Alvernon Road in north Tucson. Trail heads due north out of parking area through desert scrub, for just over a mile, to Finger Rock Spring. Keep in mind you will start to climb noticeably just past the spring; this is your way of knowing you are still on trail and not following canyon bottom.

As the trail starts to climb, you are challenged by loose rocks and dim trail to the 3-mile mark, where there is a nice view of Finger Rock on your left. Watch for good views of Tucson over your right shoulder.

It is now 1.5 miles to an intersection over somewhat better trail, still climbing, of course, but not as steep. At the intersection a right turn travels to Ventana Canyon, Esperero, and Sabino Canyon Trails and more. Trail to left is Finger Rock Trail where trail's end and the Mt. Kimball peak is only .5 mile away.

Very nice views are to be had from Mt. Kimball, as well as many choices for more hiking from here.

FINGER ROCK TRAIL

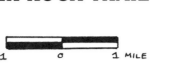

1 0 1 MILE

MT. KIMBALL

PIMA CYN. TR. ×7255' VENTANA
ESPERERO
SABINO CYN.

ROCK CANYON

FINGER ROCK
SPRING

FINGER ROCK TRAIL

FINGER

3050' ×

PONTATOC CANYON
& RIDGE TRAILS

ALVERNON

Ⓟ

SWAN

SKYLINE DR.

WINTER SPRING SUMMER FALL

▭▭	HARD SURFACE	ᵕᵕᴼ SPRING
══	LIGHT DUTY	⅄⅄⅄ RIM
═════	UNIMPROVED	ᴗ CORRAL
-----	TRAIL	× PEAK
++++	RAILROAD	Ⓟ TRAILHEAD
■ ■	BUILDINGS	P. PARKING
○	WATER TANK	☁ WATER
▲	CAMPSITE	～ RIVER
×5270	ELEVATION CHECK	～...～. DRAINAGE

VENTANA CANYON TRAIL

ATTRACTION: The "Window" at 7000' with a 25' opening; beware of 100' dropoff here

REQUIREMENTS: 3.5 hours hiking time one way; food, water, rain gear, map

LOCATION: Santa Catalina Mountains, Tucson

DIFFICULTY: Moderate to difficult

ELEVATIONS: 3100'-7000'

LENGTH: 6.4 miles one way

MAPS REQUIRED: Santa Catalina Mountain Trail and Recreation map, basic 15 minute series, U.S. Forest Service

PERMIT : No

BIKES : No

EQUESTRIAN : Not recommended

WATER: Most of the way; purify

INFORMATION: Area before trailhead on private property; access could be denied at any time; check at Visitor Center

FIREARMS: Yes

PETS ON LEASH: First 2.4 miles only

TRAIL INFORMATION

Inquire at the Sabino Canyon Visitor Center for accessibility. Park at Ventana Canyon Resort and travel on foot, via dirt road, to the Flying V Guest Ranch. Travel on the south side of the ranch via gravel road across and up Ventana Canyon to the end of the road and the trailhead.

It will be about 2.5 miles until you get into forest and away from the desert scrub. During this stretch, pay very close attention to the trail as you can get lost easily. Eventually, you will switchback up to a saddle of sorts, only to drop down to the creek again at Maiden Pools. This is a cozy camping area with an occasional waterfall.

From here travel up the canyon close to the creek. Just under 2.5 miles from Maiden Pools, towards the end of the canyon, you will encounter a series of switchbacks which will take you out of the canyon to an intersection just beyond the 5-mile mark. Mt. Kimball is to the left, Ventana Trail and the Window to the right. This last 1.2 miles of trail are a stiff climb of just under 1000'. Watch your footing around the Window, which is the end of the trail.

VENTANA CANYON TRAIL

1   0   1 MILE

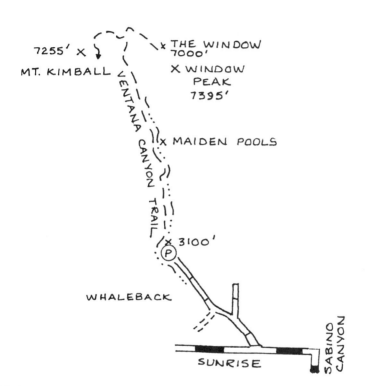

7255' X
MT. KIMBALL

X THE WINDOW
7000'

X WINDOW
PEAK
7395'

VENTANA CANYON TRAIL

X MAIDEN POOLS

X 3100'
(P)

WHALEBACK

SABINO CANYON

SUNRISE

W
I
N
T
E
R
S
P
R
I
N
G
S
U
M
M
E
R
F
A
L
L

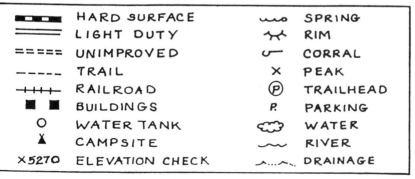

▬▭▬ HARD SURFACE		⌒o SPRING	
═══ LIGHT DUTY		⤣⤣ RIM	
===== UNIMPROVED		⌐ CORRAL	
----- TRAIL		X PEAK	
++++ RAILROAD		(P) TRAILHEAD	
■ ■ BUILDINGS		P. PARKING	
O WATER TANK		☁ WATER	
▲ CAMPSITE		⌒ RIVER	
X5270 ELEVATION CHECK		⌒...⌒ DRAINAGE	

PHONE LINE TRAIL

ATTRACTION: Easy trail; several side trips are possible; study your map

REQUIREMENTS: 2 hours hiking time one way; food, water, rain gear, map

LOCATION: Santa Catalina Mountains, Tucson

DIFFICULTY: Easy

ELEVATIONS: 2720'-3600'-3280'

LENGTH: 4.7 miles one way

MAPS REQUIRED: Santa Catalina Mountain Trail and Recreation map, basic 15 minute series, U.S. Forest Service

PERMIT : No

BIKES : No

EQUESTRIAN : Moderate to easy—narrow places with soft shoulders

WATER: Yes, purify

INFORMATION: Fine views of Sabino Canyon

FIREARMS: No

PETS ON LEASH: No

TRAIL INFORMATION

Trailhead can be reached by taking tram from the Sabino Canyon Visitor Center, less than a mile, to the Lower Sabino Canyon recreation area, or you can hike the .8 mile on pavement. Trailhead will be obvious at the bridge.

In just over .5 mile, after minimal climbing, an intersection will be encountered where Blackett Ridge Trail takes off to the right and dead ends in just over 2 miles.

The Phone Line Trail continues straight as you gently climb just under a mile to another intersection. A left turn here descends to Sabino creek; continue straight. It is also a gentle climb for the next 3.2 miles to trail's end, most of which you will be high above the creek.

Here there is another intersection where Sabino Canyon Trail goes straight ahead, or you can turn left, going downhill for about .5 mile to the end of Upper Sabino Canyon Road. You can build your own hike from this point.

PHONE LINE TRAIL

TRUE NORTH

1 0 1 MILE

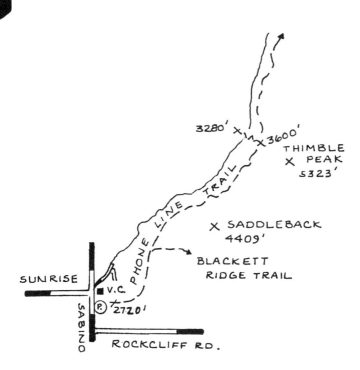

3280' X
X 3600'
THIMBLE
X PEAK
5323'

PHONE LINE TRAIL

X SADDLEBACK
4409'

BLACKETT
RIDGE TRAIL

SUNRISE

V.C.

P. 2720'

SABINO

ROCKCLIFF RD.

WINTER SPRING SUMMER FALL

▬▬▬	HARD SURFACE	⌣⌣o SPRING
══════	LIGHT DUTY	⋏⋏⋏ RIM
=====	UNIMPROVED	⌣ CORRAL
------	TRAIL	X PEAK
++++	RAILROAD	Ⓟ TRAILHEAD
■ ■	BUILDINGS	P. PARKING
O	WATER TANK	☁ WATER
▲	CAMPSITE	～ RIVER
X5270	ELEVATION CHECK	～...～ DRAINAGE

BEAR CANYON TRAIL

ATTRACTION: At 2.2 miles is Seven Falls side trip; study your map for other trail possibilities

REQUIREMENTS: 4 hours hiking time one way; food, water, rain gear, map

LOCATION: Santa Catalina Mountains, Tucson

DIFFICULTY: Easy to moderate

ELEVATIONS: 2800'-4800'-3680'

LENGTH: 8.6 miles one way

MAPS REQUIRED: Santa Catalina Mountain Trail and Recreation map, basic 15 minute series, U.S. Forest Service

PERMIT : No

BIKES : No

EQUESTRIAN : Moderate

WATER: Not dependable

INFORMATION: Either walk 1.7 miles to trailhead or take tram from Sabino Canyon Visitor Center

FIREARMS: No

PETS ON LEASH: No

TRAIL INFORMATION

Trailhead can be reached by taking the tram from the Sabino Canyon Visitor Center for just under 2 miles.

The trail skirts Bear Creek for first 2 miles. You will cross the creek several times via handmade stepping stones. As the massive cliffs close in, you will come to a couple of switchbacks which take the trail to about 100' above the creek. At about 2 miles, a small trail takes off to the left for .2 mile leading to Seven Falls, well worth seeing during wet periods. Bear Canyon Trail continues to the right.

Trail continues up the canyon above the creek (nice view of the falls). After crossing creek, prepare for some switchbacking. Trail now gets easier and continues to an old intersection at Thimble Saddle. The correct trail is obvious, to the left.

Trail is mostly downhill now and very distinct for the next mile. You will reach Palisade trailhead at Pine Creek. Palisade Trail is to the right; continue straight. Bear Canyon Trail ends just after the right turn for Box Camp Trail. At the main intersection, West Fork Trail continues straight ahead, or turn left on Sabino Canyon Trail.

BEAR CANYON TRAIL

TRUE NORTH

1   0   1 MILE

WINTER SPRING SUMMER FALL

WEST FORK TR.   BOX CAMP TR.   PALISADE TR.

SABINO CYN. TR.   3680' X

4800' X   SYCAMORE CYN.

X

SEVEN FALLS

BEAR CANYON TRAIL

SUNRISE

2800' X

P

V.C.

P.

SABINO

ROCKCLIFF

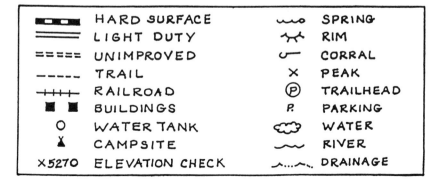

▬▬▬	HARD SURFACE	⌒○	SPRING
═══	LIGHT DUTY	⋏⋏	RIM
═════	UNIMPROVED	⌔	CORRAL
-----	TRAIL	×	PEAK
++++	RAILROAD	Ⓟ	TRAILHEAD
■ ■	BUILDINGS	P.	PARKING
○	WATER TANK	⌬	WATER
⚊	CAMPSITE	⌒	RIVER
×5270	ELEVATION CHECK	⌒...⌒	DRAINAGE

ASPEN DRAW TRAIL

ATTRACTION: Fantastic views; something to do from ski area if you are not a skier

REQUIREMENTS: 3/4 hour hiking time one way; food, water, rain gear, map

LOCATION: Santa Catalina Mountains, Tucson

DIFFICULTY: Easy

ELEVATIONS: 8940'-8400'

LENGTH: 1.6 miles one way

MAPS REQUIRED: Santa Catalina Mountain Trail and Recreation map, basic 15 minute series, U.S. Forest Service

PERMIT : No

BIKES : No

EQUESTRIAN : No

WATER: No

INFORMATION: Works well to take tram to ski area then hike back down

FIREARMS: Yes

PETS ON LEASH: Yes

TRAIL INFORMATION

Take the Mt. Lemmon Highway out of Tucson into the Catalinas, past Summerhaven to the ski area and tram. Just because you might not ski does not mean you can't have fun here. Take the tram to the top and you will find the trailhead.

Trail heads east from here and skirts the area above as you descend. The trail winds through thick forest (mostly aspen) and eventually forms a horseshoe and heads west towards the end at the tram where you started. It is a very enjoyable round trip.

There are other options in this area.

ASPEN DRAW TRAIL

0   ½   1 MILE

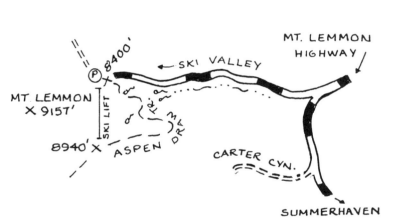

8400'

MT. LEMMON
X 9157'

← SKI VALLEY

MT. LEMMON
HIGHWAY

SKI LIFT

8940' X   ASPEN DRAW

CARTER CYN.

SUMMERHAVEN

WINTER SPRING SUMMER FALL

	HARD SURFACE		SPRING
	LIGHT DUTY	⅄	RIM
=====	UNIMPROVED	⌒	CORRAL
-----	TRAIL	X	PEAK
+++	RAILROAD	Ⓟ	TRAILHEAD
■ ■	BUILDINGS	P.	PARKING
O	WATER TANK	☁	WATER
▲	CAMPSITE	～	RIVER
X5270	ELEVATION CHECK	～...～	DRAINAGE

BUTTERFLY TRAIL

ATTRACTION: A lot of unusual varieties of plant growth; nice views

REQUIREMENTS: 3 hours hiking time one way; food, water, rain gear, map

LOCATION: Santa Catalina Mountains, Tucson

DIFFICULTY: Moderate to difficult

ELEVATIONS: 7680'-8350'-7950'

LENGTH: 5.7 miles one way

MAPS REQUIRED: Santa Catalina Mountain Trail and Recreation map, basic 15 minute series, U.S. Forest Service

PERMIT : No

BIKES : Yes

EQUESTRIAN : Moderate; some narrow areas

WATER: Yes, except during dry months

INFORMATION: Connects Soldier Camp with Palisade Ranger Station

FIREARMS: Yes

PETS ON LEASH: Yes

TRAIL INFORMATION

Trailhead is at the gravel road turnoff to Soldier Camp from the Mt. Lemmon Highway. The trail starts out on this road and follows it for about .2 mile just before it turns into a regular foot trail.

From here to Crystal Spring Trail intersection, at the 1.4 mile mark, is a section with a fair amount of altitude loss. At this intersection, Crystal Spring is to the left; continue straight.

For the next 1.8 miles, you transverse some switchbacks to about the Novio Spring area and lose about 300' in altitude, only to gain it and more back from the spring to the Davis Spring Trail intersection. Davis Spring is to the left; continue straight.

The next section of trail (2 miles) is the most difficult with over a 1200' altitude gain to a saddle just east of the Mt. Bigelow Towers. At this intersection the radio towers, Mt. Bigelow and the fire tower are to your right. From here, continue straight for next .5 mile as trail drops down to end of trail at Palisade Ranger Station on Mt. Lemmon Highway.

See how many varieties of plant growth you can pick out on this hike; there are a lot!

BUTTERFLY TRAIL

0   ½   1 MILE

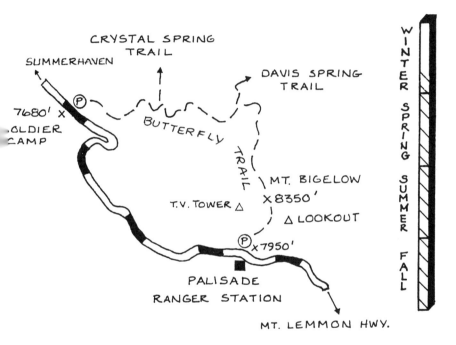

CRYSTAL SPRING
TRAIL

SUMMERHAVEN

DAVIS SPRING
TRAIL

7680' X
SOLDIER
CAMP

BUTTERFLY TRAIL

MT. BIGELOW
X 8350'

T.V. TOWER △

△ LOOKOUT

x 7950'

PALISADE
RANGER STATION

MT. LEMMON HWY.

WINTER SPRING SUMMER FALL

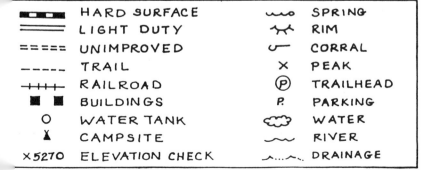

HARD SURFACE	SPRING	
LIGHT DUTY	RIM	
UNIMPROVED	CORRAL	
TRAIL	PEAK	
RAILROAD	Ⓟ TRAILHEAD	
BUILDINGS	P. PARKING	
O WATER TANK	WATER	
▲ CAMPSITE	RIVER	
X5270 ELEVATION CHECK	DRAINAGE	

NO NAME TRAIL

ATTRACTION: Makes possible a loop hike to visit Mt. Kimball, the Window and Window Peak, then back down

REQUIREMENTS: 2 hours hiking time one way; food, water, rain gear, map

LOCATION: Santa Catalina Mountains, Tucson

DIFFICULTY: Moderate to difficult

ELEVATIONS: 6880'-6080'

LENGTH: 1.8 miles one way

MAPS REQUIRED: Santa Catalina Mountain Trail and Recreation map, basic 15 minute series, U.S. Forest Service

PERMIT : No

BIKES : No

EQUESTRIAN : Not recommended

WATER: No

INFORMATION: There seems to be a lot of confusion on the name of this trail; just keep in mind it connects Mt. Kimball Trail to Ventana Canyon Trail

FIREARMS: Yes

PETS ON LEASH: No

TRAIL INFORMATION

Trailhead is found at an intersection .5 mile below the summit, towards the upper end of Finger Rock Trail. A left turn here would take you to Mt. Kimball and its peak.

The trail turns right at this intersection with switchbacks immediately. You have quite a bit of altitude to lose on this trail. Please be advised that, while I am preparing this, the trail is horribly overgrown but was slated to be worked on in the summer of 1992. Just in case, take your topo map and compass and know how to use them.

Study your map; realize your projected directions. Notice also that the trail almost levels until you turn and head east at about the halfway point, and sharply drops to the end where it intersects with Ventana Canyon Trail.

This trail creates a lot of trail options in this area.

NO NAME TRAIL

0   ½   1 MILE

WINTER SPRING SUMMER FALL

(TRAIL
N O N A M E

MT. KIMBALL
× 7255'

×6080' WINDOW
PEAK

PIMA
CANYON
TRAIL

× 6880'

VENTANA
CANYON TRAIL

FINGER ROCK
TRAIL

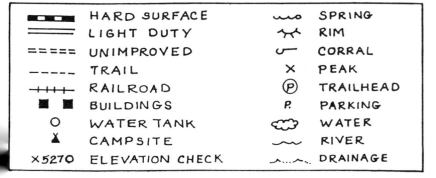

▬▬▬	HARD SURFACE	⌒⌒o	SPRING
═══	LIGHT DUTY	⋎⋎	RIM
=====	UNIMPROVED	⌒	CORRAL
-----	TRAIL	×	PEAK
++++	RAILROAD	Ⓟ	TRAILHEAD
■ ■	BUILDINGS	P.	PARKING
O	WATER TANK	⌬	WATER
▲	CAMPSITE	⌇	RIVER
×5270	ELEVATION CHECK	⌇...⌇	DRAINAGE

CATHEDRAL ROCK TRAIL

ATTRACTION: This trail connects the front range to the upper range to anywhere in the high country

REQUIREMENTS: 1.5 hours hiking time one way; food, water, rain gear, map

LOCATION: Santa Catalina Mountains, Tucson

DIFFICULTY: Moderate to difficult

ELEVATIONS: 6080'-5520'

LENGTH: 2.9 miles one way

MAPS REQUIRED: Santa Catalina Mountain Trail and Recreation map, basic 15 minute series, U.S. Forest Service

PERMIT : No

BIKES : No

EQUESTRIAN : Not recommended

WATER: No

INFORMATION: The Spur Trail that goes to Cathedral Rock is mostly used by people who want to climb it; we are talking hard rock climbing.

FIREARMS: Yes

PETS ON LEASH: No

TRAIL INFORMATION

Trailhead is located on the upper end of the Esperero Canyon Trail, just 2 miles short of the Window.

Trail takes off to the right and, for the first 1.1 miles, climbs rather steeply through some overgrowth and loose, unstable footing. Here is the Spur Trail to Cathedral Rock. Main trail continues straight and over the same kind of terrain. You will lose more altitude than you had gained to the Spur Trail before intersecting the Mt. Lemmon Trail at the end.

A right turn heads to Sabino Basin and a left turn heads into endless possibilities, even Mt. Lemmon.

CATHEDRAL ROCK TRAIL

0   ½   1 MILE

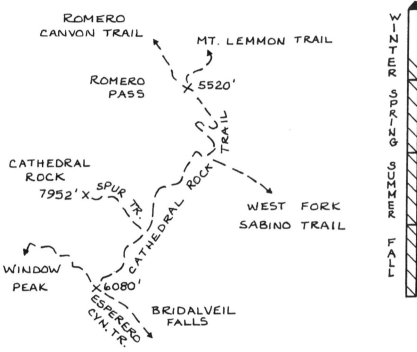

▄▄▄ HARD SURFACE	ᔕᴏ	SPRING
═══ LIGHT DUTY	ᑕᏆ	RIM
═════ UNIMPROVED	ᔓ	CORRAL
───── TRAIL	×	PEAK
┼┼┼ RAILROAD	Ⓟ	TRAILHEAD
■ ■ BUILDINGS	P.	PARKING
O WATER TANK	☁	WATER
⚑ CAMPSITE	～	RIVER
×5270 ELEVATION CHECK	～...～	DRAINAGE

ROMERO CANYON TRAIL

ATTRACTION: A very popular trail to the high country from Catalina State Park with swimming holes and great camping and scenery

REQUIREMENTS: 4 hours hiking time one way; food, water, rain gear, map

LOCATION: Santa Catalina Mountains, Tucson

DIFFICULTY: Moderate to difficult

ELEVATIONS: 2840'-6050'

LENGTH: 7 miles one way

MAPS REQUIRED: Santa Catalina Mountain Trail and Recreation map, basic 15 minute series, U.S. Forest Service

PERMIT : No

BIKES : Yes

EQUESTRIAN : Moderate with some hazardous sections

WATER: Not dependable

INFORMATION: Catalina State Park can advise you of any changes in the trailhead conditions; it is in their State Park

FIREARMS: Yes

PETS ON LEASH: Yes

TRAIL INFORMATION

Trailhead can be found by heading north out of Tucson on Oracle Road to Catalina State Park. When entering, continue to the end of the paved road, always staying to the right.

Trail starts easy and stays easy while in the park. Watch for a trail intersection at .6-mile mark where Canyon Loop Trail turns left with some easy possibilities for the whole family within the park. Romero Canyon Trail continues straight and, after a long mile into the hike, you enter Coronado National Forest. As your map indicates, the terrain changes drastically. From where you entered the forest to just under the 3-mile mark, just before you drop into Romero Canyon, you will have gained just under 1000'. You will travel through some rocky areas.

You will encounter swimming holes. Trail zigzags up the canyon. Eventually you will travel up the side of Romero Canyon to enjoy a few flat areas, only to drop down into the canyon again. You will zigzag the canyon several more times for over a mile but

ROMERO CANYON TRAIL

1   0   1 MILE

ORACLE

CANYON LOOP TR.

P×
2840'

CATALINA ST. PK

ROMERO CYN. TR.

MONTROSE CANYON

ROMERO PASS

× 6050'

WINTER SPRING SUMMER FALL

ORACLE ROAD

HARD SURFACE		SPRING
LIGHT DUTY		RIM
UNIMPROVED		CORRAL
TRAIL		× PEAK
RAILROAD		Ⓟ TRAILHEAD
BUILDINGS		P. PARKING
O WATER TANK		WATER
CAMPSITE		RIVER
×5270 ELEVATION CHECK		DRAINAGE

Arizona South / 91

BOX CAMP TRAIL

ATTRACTION: Nice areas for camping a little over 5 miles into the trail

REQUIREMENTS: 5 hours hiking time one way; food, water, rain gear, map

LOCATION: Santa Catalina Mountains, Tucson

DIFFICULTY: Moderate to difficult

ELEVATIONS: 3760'-8040'

LENGTH: 7.1 miles one way

MAPS REQUIRED: Santa Catalina Mountain Trail and Recreation map, basic 15 minute series, U.S. Forest Service

PERMIT : No

BIKES : No

EQUESTRIAN : Moderate to difficult

WATER: Not dependable

INFORMATION: This is another trail on which you will not want to forget your topo map and compass; can be overgrown; areas of loose footing; know your limits

FIREARMS: Yes

PETS ON LEASH: Yes

TRAIL INFORMATION

Trailhead is located in Sabino Basin only 100 yards east of the upper end of Sabino Canyon Trail.

This trail heads almost due north and, in the next 2.3 miles, a lot of altitude is to be gained, via some loose footing and some switchbacks, before arriving at Apache Spring (dependable only in wet conditions). You will continue to switchback from the spring but, in spite of this, the trail is a little easier.

In just over 5 miles, a small intersection is encountered and a left turn here takes you to Box Spring in about 1/4 mile. You should continue straight at this intersection and head up Spencer Canyon. The trail gets easier again as you progress to the Mt. Lemmon Highway at trail's end. Fine views are to be enjoyed along this trail.

There is fine camping at Soldier Camp and Bear Wallow Campground just north of trail's end or, closer yet, in Spencer Canyon to the south.

BOX CAMP TRAIL

1   0   1 MILE

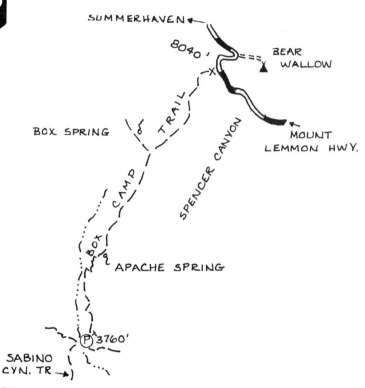

SUMMERHAVEN

8040'

BEAR WALLOW

BOX SPRING

BOX CAMP TRAIL

SPENCER CANYON

MOUNT LEMMON HWY.

APACHE SPRING

P 3760'

SABINO CYN. TR →

WINTER SPRING SUMMER FALL

	HARD SURFACE		SPRING
	LIGHT DUTY		RIM
=====	UNIMPROVED		CORRAL
-----	TRAIL	×	PEAK
++++	RAILROAD	Ⓟ	TRAILHEAD
■ ■	BUILDINGS	P.	PARKING
O	WATER TANK		WATER
▲	CAMPSITE		RIVER
×5270	ELEVATION CHECK		DRAINAGE

DOUGLAS SPRING TRAIL

ATTRACTION: Magnificent views of the high country

REQUIREMENTS: 5 hours hiking time one way; food, water, rain gear, maps

LOCATION: West-Central Rincon Mountains; Saguaro National Monument East, Tucson

DIFFICULTY: Moderate

ELEVATIONS: 2749' to 6120' to 5400'

LENGTH: 9.7 miles one way

MAPS REQUIRED: Tanque Verde Peak Quadrangle, Pima County; Mica Mountain Quadrangle, Pima County; 7.5 minute series topographic

PERMIT: If you camp overnight

BIKES: No

EQUESTRIAN: Yes

WATER: No, Douglas Spring not dependable nor is Tina Larga Tank at 3 miles.

INFORMATION: Permit available at Saguaro National Monument East, Tucson

FIREARMS: No

PETS ON LEASH: No

TRAIL INFORMATION

Trail begins at the end of East Speedway Road next to the Ramada. This trail climbs slowly but surely over minor ups and downs for the first 6 miles to Douglas Spring Campground, with an altitude gain of only about 1900' over gently rolling lower desert.

For about the next 2.5 miles to Cow Head Saddle, the trail becomes steeper as you near the saddle, incorporating only a few switchbacks. At 6120', Cow Head Saddle is a 4-way intersection with Douglas Spring Trail continuing straight ahead.

Trail then drops down for about 1.5 miles, ending at Manning Camp Trail at 5400'. Here a left turn takes you to Grass Shack Campground, a good place to spend the night.

DOUGLAS SPRING TRAIL

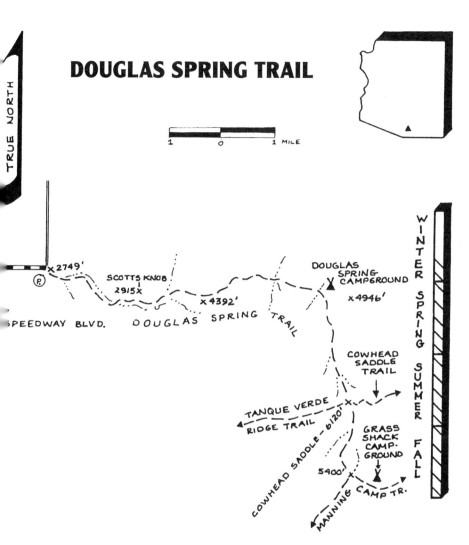

1 | 0 | 1 MILE

TRUE NORTH

WINTER SPRING SUMMER FALL

X 2749'
(P)
SCOTTS KNOB
2915X
X 4392'
SPEEDWAY BLVD.   DOUGLAS SPRING TRAIL
DOUGLAS SPRING CAMPGROUND
X 4946'
COWHEAD SADDLE TRAIL
TANQUE VERDE RIDGE TRAIL
COWHEAD SADDLE - 6120'
GRASS SHACK CAMP. GROUND
5400'
MANNING CAMP TR.

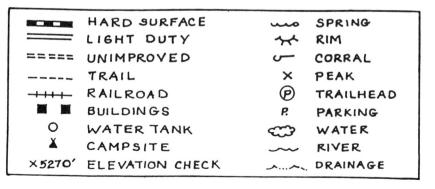

▬▬	HARD SURFACE	ᨆ	SPRING
═══	LIGHT DUTY	〽	RIM
=====	UNIMPROVED	ↄ	CORRAL
-----	TRAIL	X	PEAK
++++	RAILROAD	Ⓟ	TRAILHEAD
■ ■	BUILDINGS	P.	PARKING
O	WATER TANK	☁	WATER
▲	CAMPSITE	∼	RIVER
X5270'	ELEVATION CHECK	∼⋯∼	DRAINAGE

MANNING CAMP TRAIL

ATTRACTION: Views of Rincon Valley and the transition zones of the plantlife along the trail.

REQUIREMENTS: 6.5 hours hiking time one way; food, water, rain gear, map

LOCATION: Central and Eastern Rincon Mountains; Saguaro National Monument East, Tucson

DIFFICULTY: Moderate to difficult

ELEVATIONS: 3400' to 7950'

LENGTH: 9.3 miles one way

MAPS REQUIRED: Mica Mountain Quadrangle, Pima County; 7.5 minute series topographic

PERMIT: If you camp overnight

BIKES: No

EQUESTRIAN: Yes

WATER: In small drainages and at Grass Shack Campground only in wet seasons; always at Manning Camp

INFORMATION: Permit available at Saguaro National Monument East, Tucson

FIREARMS: No

PETS ON LEASH: No

TRAIL INFORMATION

Be advised that there is no public access nor any camping at Madrona Ranger Station; you may only pass through! The only way to enter is by hiking down the very geologic Rincon Creek Trail from Happy Valley Campground.

Manning Camp Trail starts north out of Madrona, rather gently at first, through lower desert and, in just over 4 miles, Douglas Spring Trail will "T" in from the left. Continue straight ahead and in about .5 mile you will come to Grass Shack Campground.

Trail will now start to climb a bit more and, in the next 3.5 miles, the flora will increase as the Devil's Bathtub Trail "T's" in from the right (a neat side trip to a 50' waterfall in rainy season or during snowmelt). Continue straight at this "T" and in only 1 mile you will arrive at Manning Camp with excellent camping and lots of water. Of course, this trip could be reversed.

MANNING CAMP TRAIL

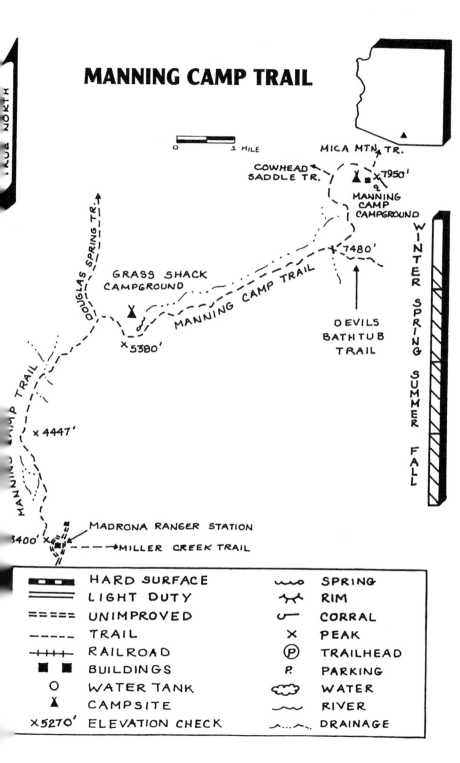

MICA MTN. TR.

COWHEAD
SADDLE TR.

X 7950'

MANNING
CAMP
CAMPGROUND

X 7480'

DOUGLAS SPRING TR.

GRASS SHACK
CAMPGROUND

MANNING CAMP TRAIL

X 5380'

DEVILS
BATHTUB
TRAIL

WINTER SPRING SUMMER FALL

MANNING CAMP TRAIL

X 4447'

MADRONA RANGER STATION

3400' X

MILLER CREEK TRAIL

▬▭▬	HARD SURFACE	ᴗᴗo	SPRING
═══	LIGHT DUTY	⅄	RIM
═════	UNIMPROVED	ᴗ	CORRAL
-----	TRAIL	×	PEAK
┼┼┼┼	RAILROAD	Ⓟ	TRAILHEAD
■ ■	BUILDINGS	P.	PARKING
O	WATER TANK	☁	WATER
⅄	CAMPSITE	～	RIVER
×5270'	ELEVATION CHECK	～...～	DRAINAGE

SWITCHBACK TRAIL

ATTRACTION: Shortcut to upper Heartbreak Ridge Trail from East Slope Trail

REQUIREMENTS: Half hour hiking time one way; food, water, rain gear, map

LOCATION: East end of the Rincon Mountains; Saguaro National Monument East, Tucson

DIFFICULTY: Difficult

ELEVATIONS: 7550' to 7820'

LENGTH: .3 mile one way

MAPS REQUIRED: Mica Mountain Quadrangle, Pima County; 7.5 minute series topographic

PERMIT: If you camp overnight

BIKES: No

EQUESTRIAN: Yes

WATER: No

INFORMATION: Permit available at Saguaro National Monument East, Tucson

FIREARMS: No

PETS ON LEASH: No

TRAIL INFORMATION

When traveling south on East Slope Trail headed for Manning Camp, this trail saves you from having to travel all the way to the four-corners area to connect with Heartbreak Ridge Trail.

Trail starts out being rather easy but the second half lives up to its name, as all the switchbacks seem to appear from out of nowhere.

Trail saves you a lot of hiking distance.

SWITCHBACK TRAIL

0   1/4 MILE

HEART BREAK RIDGE TRAIL

EAST SLOPE TRAIL

7820'

7550'

SWITCHBACK TRAIL

WINTER SPRING SUMMER FALL

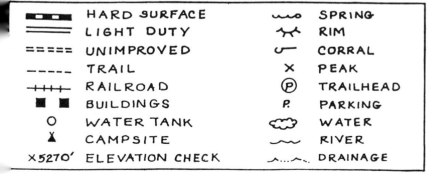

■ ▬ ■ HARD SURFACE	⌒o	SPRING
═══════ LIGHT DUTY	⋎⋎	RIM
===== UNIMPROVED	⌒	CORRAL
– – – – – TRAIL	✕	PEAK
+++++ RAILROAD	ⓟ	TRAILHEAD
■ ■ BUILDINGS	P.	PARKING
O WATER TANK	⌣⌣⌣	WATER
▲ CAMPSITE	⌒⌒	RIVER
✕5270' ELEVATION CHECK	⌒...⌒	DRAINAGE

NORTH SLOPE TRAIL

ATTRACTION: Magnificent views; seclusion

REQUIREMENTS: 1.5 hours hiking time one way; food, water, rain gear, map

LOCATION: Central area of the Rincon Mountains; Saguaro National Monument East, Tucson

DIFFICULTY: Moderate

ELEVATIONS: 8150' to 8450'

LENGTH: 3 miles one way

MAPS REQUIRED: Mica Mountain Quadrangle, Pima County; 7.5 minute series topographic

PERMIT: If you camp overnight

BIKES: No

EQUESTRIAN: Yes

WATER: At Italian Spring (small side trip) unless drought conditions

INFORMATION: Permit available at Saguaro National Monument East, Tucson

FIREARMS: No

PETS ON LEASH: No

TRAIL INFORMATION

When camped at Manning Camp, this trail, along with Cow Head Saddle Trail, East Slope Trail and a small portion of Heartbreak Ridge Trail, makes for an adventurous day's hike.

This trail is very secluded with an excellent view of Helen's Dome at 8364'. The views of the valley below to the northwest are absolutely awesome!

Trail is easy to follow and, because of the deep cover of pine needles, you can hardly hear your own footsteps. It is a favorite trail of mine.

NORTH SLOPE TRAIL

0   1 MILE

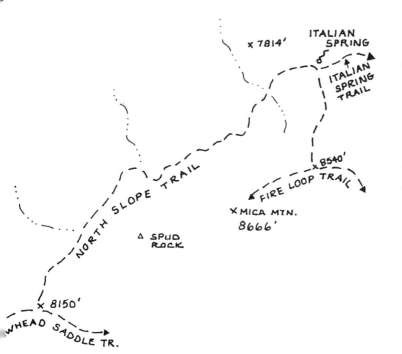

x 7814'

ITALIAN
SPRING

ITALIAN
SPRING
TRAIL

NORTH SLOPE TRAIL

x 8540'

FIRE LOOP TRAIL

x MICA MTN.
8666'

△ SPUD
ROCK

x 8150'

WHEAD SADDLE TR.

WINTER SPRING SUMMER FALL

▭	HARD SURFACE	ᵕᵕo SPRING
═══	LIGHT DUTY	⋌⋋⋋ RIM
=====	UNIMPROVED	⌣ CORRAL
- - - -	TRAIL	✕ PEAK
+++++	RAILROAD	Ⓟ TRAILHEAD
■ ■	BUILDINGS	P. PARKING
○	WATER TANK	☁ WATER
▲	CAMPSITE	∼∼ RIVER
✕5270'	ELEVATION CHECK	∼...∼ DRAINAGE

COW HEAD SADDLE TRAIL

ATTRACTION: Popular route to Manning Camp from Saguaro National Monument East, along with Douglas Spring Trail

REQUIREMENTS: 2.5 hours hiking time one way; food, water, rain gear, map

LOCATION: Central area of the Rincon Mountains; Saguaro National Monument East, Tucson

DIFFICULTY: Moderate to difficult

ELEVATIONS: 6120' to 7950'

LENGTH: 4 miles one way

MAPS REQUIRED: Mica Mountain Quadrangle, Pima County; 7.5 minute series topographic

PERMIT: If you camp overnight

BIKES: No

EQUESTRIAN: Yes

WATER: At Manning Camp at 7950'

INFORMATION: Permit available at Saguaro National Monument East, Tucson

FIREARMS: No

PETS ON LEASH: No

TRAIL INFORMATION

This trail, along with Douglas Spring Trail, provides the shortest route from Saguaro National Monument East to Manning Camp, as well as being very scenic as far as the variety of flora.

Trail starts at Cow Head Saddle intersection and travels east to Manning Camp (consult your maps).

The first 3.3 miles are very uphill while staying under a thick, shaded canopy of trees. In 3.3 miles, a marked intersection appears where North Slope Trail travels north (a very scenic trail); continue straight ahead and, in .2 mile, you will see the intersection of Fire Loop Trail. At this point your uphill travel is over. Continue straight again .4 mile to Manning Camp with excellent campsites and a lot of water.

COW HEAD SADDLE TRAIL

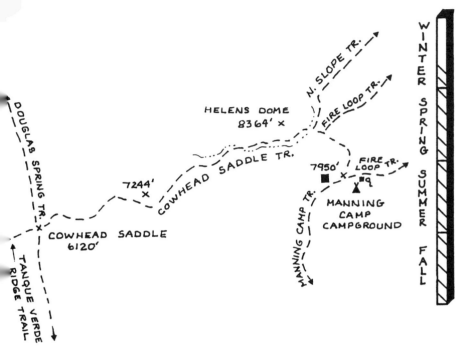

0   1 MILE

WINTER SPRING SUMMER FALL

N. SLOPE TR.

FIRE LOOP TR.

HELENS DOME
8364' ×

DOUGLAS SPRING TR.

COWHEAD SADDLE TR.

7244'
×

7950'
■

FIRE LOOP TR.
×

MANNING CAMP TR.

MANNING CAMP CAMPGROUND

COWHEAD SADDLE
6120'

TANQUE VERDE RIDGE TRAIL

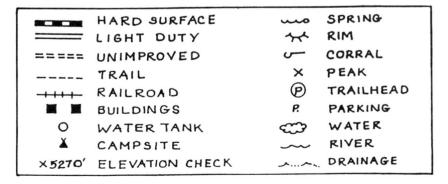

▬▬▬	HARD SURFACE	∼∽○	SPRING
══	LIGHT DUTY	⋏⋏⋎	RIM
=====	UNIMPROVED	⌣	CORRAL
-----	TRAIL	×	PEAK
++++	RAILROAD	Ⓟ	TRAILHEAD
■ ■	BUILDINGS	P.	PARKING
O	WATER TANK	☁	WATER
▲	CAMPSITE	∼	RIVER
×5270'	ELEVATION CHECK	∼…∼	DRAINAGE

EAST SLOPE TRAIL

ATTRACTION: Magnificent views; seclusion

REQUIREMENTS: 2.5 hours hiking time one way; food, water, rain gear, map

LOCATION: East end of Rincon Mountains; Saguaro National Monument East, Tucson

DIFFICULTY: Moderate to difficult

ELEVATIONS: 7580' to 6800' to 7345'

LENGTH: 4.1 miles one way

MAPS REQUIRED: Mica Mountain Quadrangle, Pima County; 7.5 minute series topographic

PERMIT: If you camp overnight

BIKES: No

EQUESTRIAN: Yes

WATER: At Spud Rock Spring unless drought conditions

INFORMATION: Permit available at Saguaro National Monument East, Tucson

FIREARMS: No

PETS ON LEASH: No

TRAIL INFORMATION

Besides the use of this trail as mentioned in information on the North Slope Trail, it is also popular as a way to travel from Mica Mountain Peak at 8666' (highest point in the Rincons) south to the four corners area.

This trail offers magnificent views of Happy Valley below and into New Mexico.

Just after coming down the switchbacks above Spud Rock Campground, the flora become dense and oftentimes a challenge. The ferns as high as your head and the many aspens surely add to a hike. Also keep in mind that this is bear country!

EAST SLOPE TRAIL

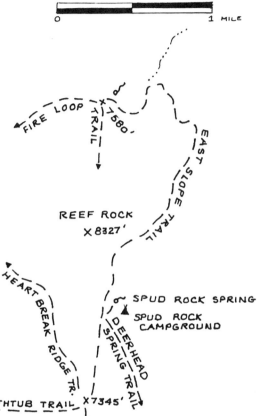

0 ———— 1 MILE

FIRE LOOP TRAIL X 7580'

EAST SLOPE TRAIL

REEF ROCK X 8327'

HEART BREAK RIDGE TR.

SPUD ROCK SPRING

SPUD ROCK CAMPGROUND

DEERHEAD SPRING TRAIL

DEVILS BATHTUB TRAIL X 7345'

WINTER SPRING SUMMER FALL

	HARD SURFACE		SPRING
	LIGHT DUTY	⌣	RIM
=====	UNIMPROVED		CORRAL
-----	TRAIL	×	PEAK
+++++	RAILROAD	Ⓟ	TRAILHEAD
■ ■	BUILDINGS	P.	PARKING
O	WATER TANK		WATER
▲	CAMPSITE		RIVER
×5270'	ELEVATION CHECK		DRAINAGE

SPUD ROCK TRAIL

ATTRACTION: Shortcut coming down Fire Loop Trail to Manning Camp

REQUIREMENTS: Half hour hiking time one way; food, water, rain gear, map

LOCATION: Central area of Rincon Mountains; Saguaro National Monument East, Tucson

DIFFICULTY: Moderate

ELEVATIONS: 8160' to 8340'

LENGTH: .5 mile one way

MAPS REQUIRED: Mica Mountain Quadrangle, Pima County; 7.5 minute series topographic

PERMIT: If you camp overnight

BIKES: No

EQUESTRIAN: Yes

WATER: No

INFORMATION: Permit available at Saguaro National Monument East, Tucson

FIREARMS: No

PETS ON LEASH: No

TRAIL INFORMATION

This trail simply serves as an alternative way down from Mica Mountain or Spud Rock itself, with less backtracking.

SPUD ROCK TRAIL

0   ½   1 MILE

SPUD ROCK
8613' x   FIRE LOOP TRAIL   MICA MTN.
              8340' + SPUD ROCK   X 8666'

                         SPUD ROCK TR.

8160' x   MICA MTN. TRAIL

MICA MEADOW

MICA MEADOW TR.

MICA

WINTER SPRING SUMMER FALL

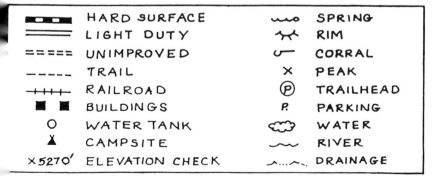

▭▭	HARD SURFACE	⌒⌒o	SPRING
═══	LIGHT DUTY	⋏⋏	RIM
═════	UNIMPROVED	⌒	CORRAL
-----	TRAIL	X	PEAK
++++	RAILROAD	Ⓟ	TRAILHEAD
■ ■	BUILDINGS	P.	PARKING
O	WATER TANK	☁	WATER
▲	CAMPSITE	∼∼	RIVER
×5270'	ELEVATION CHECK	∼...∼.	DRAINAGE

DEER HEAD SPRING TRAIL

ATTRACTION: Lush Spud Rock Campground on north end of trail, along with a stand of aspens

REQUIREMENTS: One-half hour hiking time one way; food, water, rain gear, map

LOCATION: East end of Rincon Mountains; Saguaro National Monument East, Tucson

DIFFICULTY: Easy to moderate

ELEVATIONS: 7120' to 7430'

LENGTH: 1.4 miles one way

MAPS REQUIRED: Mica Mountain Quadrangle, Pima County; 7.5 minute series topographic

PERMIT: If you camp overnight

BIKES: No

EQUESTRIAN: Yes

WATER: At Deer Head Spring unless drought conditions

INFORMATION: Permit available at Saguaro National Monument East, Tucson

FIREARMS: No

PETS ON LEASH: No

TRAIL INFORMATION

If you came up Turkey Creek Trail, it terminates midway on the north-south Deer Head Spring Trail. Traveling south, Deer Head Spring Trail terminates in .8 mile on Heartbreak Ridge Trail headed towards Happy Valley fire watch cabin.

Traveling north on Deer Head Spring Trail will lead you through a grove of aspens to where it terminates in .6 mile to East Slope Trail and Spud Rock Campground.

This trail lets you avoid a maze of trails towards your destination.

DEER HEAD SPRING TRAIL

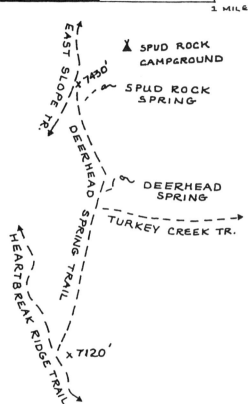

0 ————— 1 MILE

EAST SLOPE TR.

X 7430'

⚊ SPUD ROCK CAMPGROUND

SPUD ROCK SPRING

DEERHEAD SPRING TRAIL

DEERHEAD SPRING

TURKEY CREEK TR.

HEARTBREAK RIDGE TRAIL

X 7120'

WINTER SPRING SUMMER FALL

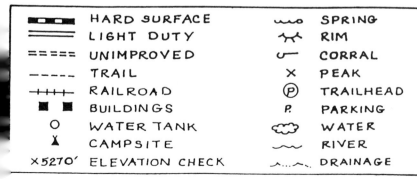

▭▭▭	HARD SURFACE	⌒⌒o	SPRING
≡≡≡	LIGHT DUTY	ᛜᛜ	RIM
=====	UNIMPROVED	⌣	CORRAL
-----	TRAIL	✕	PEAK
++++	RAILROAD	Ⓟ	TRAILHEAD
■ ■	BUILDINGS	P.	PARKING
O	WATER TANK	☁	WATER
⚊	CAMPSITE	⌇	RIVER
✕5270'	ELEVATION CHECK	⌁...⌁	DRAINAGE

TANQUE VERDE TRAIL

ATTRACTION: Tanque Verde Peak views; transition zones
REQUIREMENTS: 6.5 hours hiking time one way; food, water, rain gear, maps
LOCATION: West-Central Rincon Mountains; Saguaro National Monument East, Tucson
DIFFICULTY: Difficult
ELEVATIONS: 3120' to 7049' to 6120'
LENGTH: 11.5 miles one way
MAPS REQUIRED: Tanque Verde Peak Quadrangle, Pima County; Mica Mountain Quadrangle, Pima County; 7.5 minute series topographic
PERMIT: If you camp overnight
BIKES: No
EQUESTRIAN: No
WATER: Nothing dependable
INFORMATION: Permit available at Saguaro National Monument East, Tucson
FIREARMS: No
PETS ON LEASH: No

TRAIL INFORMATION

Trailhead is found in Javelina Picnic Area in the monument at 3120'. Trail begins gently downhill (enjoy it while you can) and over a couple ups and downs to a saddle in about 1 mile. Make a left turn here at a junction at the saddle to begin a vigorous climb to Juniper Basin Campground. More often than not, you will be hiking over very steep sections of trail. When you think you have almost had it with the uphill climb, the trail levels out for almost a mile to Juniper Basin Campground, a perfect place to spend the night.

In about 2 more miles and after climbing more steep trail, a junction appears where a right turn will take you to the Summit Register, less than 10' below Tanque Verde Peak at 7049'. After enjoying the view, return to the main trail, east. The trail descends steeply at first but becomes more gentle the closer you get to Cow Head Saddle at the trail's end. Here you have several options.

Beware of rock outcroppings on trail where one can easily lose his way; take great care in these areas.

TANQUE VERDE TRAIL

1   0   1 MILE

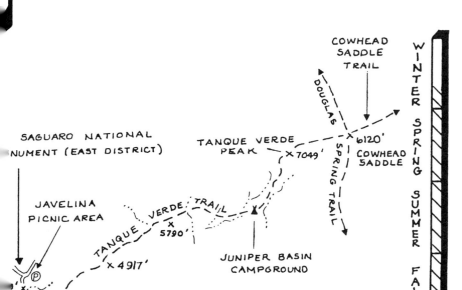

COWHEAD
SADDLE
TRAIL

DOUGLAS SPRING TRAIL

X 6120'
COWHEAD
SADDLE

WINTER SPRING SUMMER FALL

SAGUARO NATIONAL
MONUMENT (EAST DISTRICT)

TANQUE VERDE
PEAK   X 7049'

JAVELINA
PICNIC AREA

TANQUE VERDE TRAIL
X 5790'

X 4917'

JUNIPER BASIN
CAMPGROUND

P

X

X 3579'

	HARD SURFACE		SPRING
	LIGHT DUTY		RIM
=====	UNIMPROVED		CORRAL
-----	TRAIL	×	PEAK
+++	RAILROAD	Ⓟ	TRAILHEAD
■ ■	BUILDINGS	P.	PARKING
O	WATER TANK		WATER
⚊	CAMPSITE		RIVER
×5270	ELEVATION CHECK		DRAINAGE

ITALIAN SPRING TRAIL

ATTRACTION: Shortest hike to Manning Camp; magnificent views

REQUIREMENTS: 4.5 hours hiking time one way; food, water, rain gear, maps

LOCATION: North-Central Rincon Mountains; Saguaro National Monument East, Tucson

DIFFICULTY: Moderate to difficult - not for novices

ELEVATIONS: 4800' to 7980'

LENGTH: 4.8 miles one way

MAPS REQUIRED: Agua Caliente Quadrangle, Pima County; Piety Hill Quadrangle, Pima County; Mica Mountain Quadrangle, Pima County; 7.5 minute series topographic

PERMIT: If you camp overnight

BIKES: No

EQUESTRIAN: Yes

WATER: At Italian Spring unless drought conditions

INFORMATION: Permit available at Saguaro National Monument East, Tucson. 4-wheel drive only and 4 hour trip to trailhead

FIREARMS: No

PETS ON LEASH: No

TRAIL INFORMATION

Access to Italian Spring trailhead is gained only by 4-wheel drive. Head east out of Tucson on Tanque Verde Road which turns into Reddington Pass Road (dirt). From this point to the Italian Spring turnoff it is 9.6 miles. This turnoff is not marked; watch your odometer. You must travel 5 more miles to the trailhead.

It will save a lot of brutal wear and tear on your 4-wheel drive if, after 2.1 of the 5 miles, you park and hike the rest of the way. This area is marked by a large fresh water tank and a windmill and is called Italian Trap. From here it is only a 2.9-mile hike to the trailhead sign for Italian Spring Trail on a very rough road.

It is 2.3 miles from the trailhead to the Saguaro National Monument boundary, and another 2.5 miles to North Slope Trail at the end. There is no letup on this trail as it is all uphill—be prepared. From trail's end it is not far to Manning Camp, a good place to spend the night.

ITALIAN SPRING TRAIL

0   1 MILE

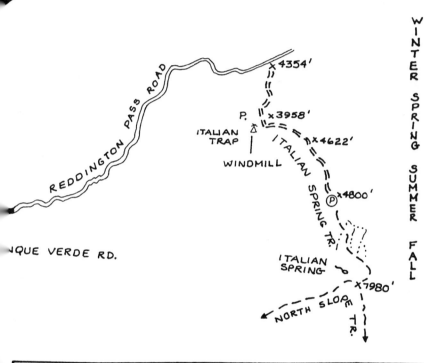

REDDINGTON PASS ROAD

x 4354'

P.

ITALIAN
TRAP

x 3958'

WINDMILL

n x 4622'

ITALIAN SPRING TR.

Ⓟ x 4800'

ITALIAN
SPRING

x 7980'

NORTH SLOPE TR.

NQUE VERDE RD.

WINTER SPRING SUMMER FALL

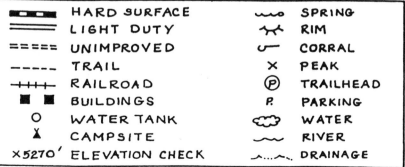

■■■	HARD SURFACE	⌒⌒o	SPRING
≡≡	LIGHT DUTY	⋏⋏	RIM
=====	UNIMPROVED	⌒	CORRAL
-----	TRAIL	×	PEAK
+++++	RAILROAD	Ⓟ	TRAILHEAD
■ ■	BUILDINGS	P.	PARKING
O	WATER TANK	☁	WATER
⚑	CAMPSITE	～	RIVER
×5270'	ELEVATION CHECK	～...～	DRAINAGE

KING CANYON TRAIL

ATTRACTION: Shortest trail to Wasson Peak; 1 mile from trailhead is an excellent picnic area called "Mam-A-Gah"; fine views

REQUIREMENTS: 2 hours hiking time one way; food, water, rain gear, map

LOCATION: Tucson Mountains, Saguaro National Monument West, Tucson

DIFFICULTY: Moderate

ELEVATIONS: 2848'-4580'

LENGTH: 3.5 miles one way

MAPS REQUIRED: Avra Quadrangle, Pima County; 7.5 minute series topographic

PERMIT: No

BIKES: No

EQUESTRIAN: Yes

WATER: No

INFORMATION: No camping, dangerous mineshaft areas, last .5 mile of trail not for a weak horse nor a novice rider, rocky

FIREARMS: No

PETS ON LEASH: No

TRAIL INFORMATION

Take Speedway west out of Tucson through Gates Pass to Kinney Road; turn right towards Desert Museum. Trailhead is in the parking area directly across from the museum.

Hike up 4-wheel drive road 100 yards to trailhead sign and information. From here it is .9 mile to the Mam-A-Gah picnic area ramada and pit toilets. Trail continues past restrooms and it crosses several washes and skirts several canyons as you slowly climb slightly. At 2.3 miles, you reach a saddle and a left turn (signed) to start your switchbacks to the end of the trail at Hugh Norris Trail.

A right turn on Hugh Norris Trail and .3 mile will take you to the summit of Wasson Peak at an altitude of 4687', a true 360-degree panorama.

KING CANYON TRAIL

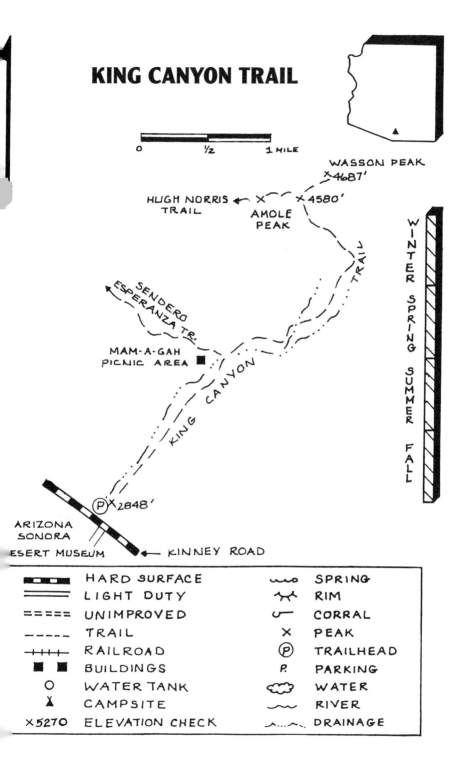

WASSON PEAK
×4687'

HUGH NORRIS ← X ~~ ×4580'
TRAIL   AMOLE
               PEAK

TRAIL

SENDERO
ESPERANZA TR.

MAM-A-GAH
PICNIC AREA ■

KING CANYON

WINTER SPRING SUMMER FALL

ⓅX2848'

ARIZONA
SONORA
ESERT MUSEUM ← KINNEY ROAD

▬▬▬	HARD SURFACE	⌒	SPRING
══	LIGHT DUTY	⋏⋏	RIM
=====	UNIMPROVED	⌣	CORRAL
-----	TRAIL	×	PEAK
++++	RAILROAD	Ⓟ	TRAILHEAD
■ ■	BUILDINGS	P.	PARKING
O	WATER TANK	☁	WATER
Ⰼ	CAMPSITE	～	RIVER
×5270	ELEVATION CHECK	⌁	DRAINAGE

HUGH NORRIS TRAIL

ATTRACTION: Center 3 miles follows ridge top with fine views to Amole Peak; ends at tallest peak in Tucson Mountains, Wasson Peak

REQUIREMENTS: 2.5 hours hiking time one way; food, water, rain gear, map

LOCATION: Tucson Mountains, Saguaro National Monument West, Tucson

DIFFICULTY: Moderate to difficult

ELEVATIONS: 2565'-4687'

LENGTH: 4.9 miles one way

MAPS REQUIRED: Avra Quadrangle, Pima County; 7.5 minute series topographic

PERMIT: No

BIKES: No

EQUESTRIAN: Yes

WATER: No

INFORMATION: No camping, dangerous mine shaft areas, last mile of trail not for a weak horse nor a novice rider, rocky

FIREARMS: No

PETS ON LEASH: No

TRAIL INFORMATION

Take Speedway west out of Tucson through Gates Pass to Kinney Road. Turn right and continue past the Red Hills Information Center at Saguaro National Monument West. The trailhead is 2.5 miles north of visitor center on the right side of Bagada Loop Drive.

Prepare for switchbacks almost the entire first mile. From here it is a ridge trail (my favorite) for approximately 3 miles, with fantastic views from the valley below to Amole Peak. About 10 more switchbacks are encountered before reaching a saddle and the intersection of King Canyon Trail. From this point it is a gentle .3 mile to end of trail at Wasson Peak, which is at an altitude of 4687'.

HUGH NORRIS TRAIL

TRUE NORTH

0 ½ 1 MILE

GOLDEN GATE RD.

TWO WAY

TWO WAY

BAJADA LOOP DRIVE

ONE WAY

ⓟ 2565'

TWO WAY

HUGH

3633'

ESPERANZA TR.

SENDERO

NORRIS TRAIL

WASSON PEAK
×
4687'

AMOLE PEAK

KING CANYON TR.

WINTER SPRING SUMMER FALL

KINNEY ROAD

■ ■ RED HILLS INFORMATION CENTER

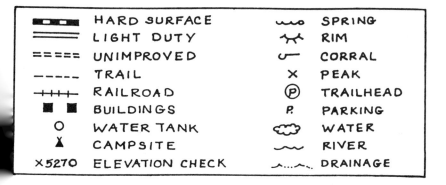

▬▬▬▬	HARD SURFACE	ᳵᵒ	SPRING
══════	LIGHT DUTY	⋏⋏	RIM
=====	UNIMPROVED	⌣	CORRAL
------	TRAIL	×	PEAK
++++	RAILROAD	ⓟ	TRAILHEAD
■ ■	BUILDINGS	P.	PARKING
O	WATER TANK	☁	WATER
▲	CAMPSITE	～	RIVER
×5270	ELEVATION CHECK	∿	DRAINAGE

SENDERO ESPERANZA TRAIL

ATTRACTION: Scenic views at intersection of Hugh Norris ridgeline; access to Wasson Peak from the north

REQUIREMENTS: 1.5 hours hiking time one way; food, water, rain gear, map

LOCATION: Tucson Mountains, Saguaro National Monument West, Tucson

DIFFICULTY: Moderate

ELEVATIONS: 2970'-3150'-2848'

LENGTH: 3.2 miles one way

MAPS REQUIRED: Avra Quadrangle, Pima County; 7.5 minute series topographic

PERMIT: No

BIKES: No

EQUESTRIAN: Yes

WATER: No

INFORMATION: No camping, first mile old mining road, dangerous mineshaft areas

FIREARMS: No

PETS ON LEASH: No

TRAIL INFORMATION

Take Speedway west out of Tucson through Gates Pass to Kinney Road; turn right here and continue past the Red Hills Information Center at Saguaro National Monument West to Golden Gate Road and turn right. Trailhead is 6 miles past information center, or 1.5 miles from intersection of Bagada Loop Drive and Golden Gate Road.

This trail ascends moderately to the ridge west of Amole and Wasson Peaks, and crosses Hugh Norris Trail at 1.8 miles with excellent views. It now descends 1.4 miles past several mineshafts (very dangerous—keep away) with fine view to the south, before terminating on the King Canyon Trail at the Mam-A-Gah picnic area. From here a .9-mile hike down King Canyon Trail brings you to the King Canyon trailhead directly across from the Desert Museum.

It would be ideal if a car were left at this trailhead on the way in to keep from having to hike back to the opposite end of Sendero Esperanza Trail.

SENDERO ESPERANZA TRAIL

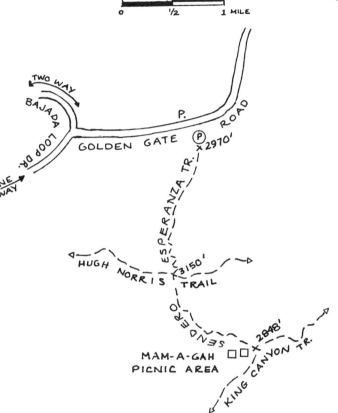

TRUE NORTH

0   ½   1 MILE

TWO WAY

BAJADA

LOOP DR.

ONE WAY

GOLDEN GATE P. ROAD

Ⓟ X 2970'

ESPERANZA TR.

HUGH NORRIS X 3150' TRAIL

SENDERO

X 2848'

MAM-A-GAH PICNIC AREA

KING CANYON TR.

WINTER SPRING SUMMER FALL

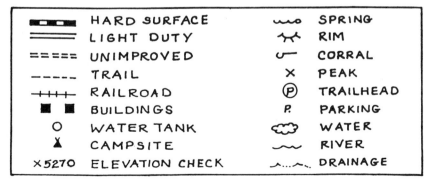

▬▭▬	HARD SURFACE	ᜐ	SPRING
═══	LIGHT DUTY	⌣	RIM
=====	UNIMPROVED	ᴗ	CORRAL
------	TRAIL	✕	PEAK
+++++	RAILROAD	Ⓟ	TRAILHEAD
■ ■	BUILDINGS	P.	PARKING
○	WATER TANK	ෆ	WATER
▲	CAMPSITE	∼	RIVER
✕5270	ELEVATION CHECK	∼...∼.	DRAINAGE

RINCON MOUNTAINS TRAILS

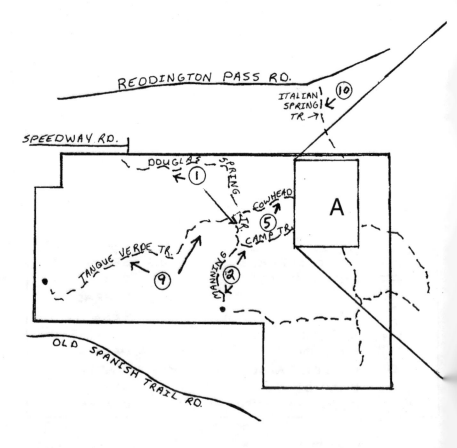

RINCON MOUNTAINS TRAILS

Expansion of "A" previous page.

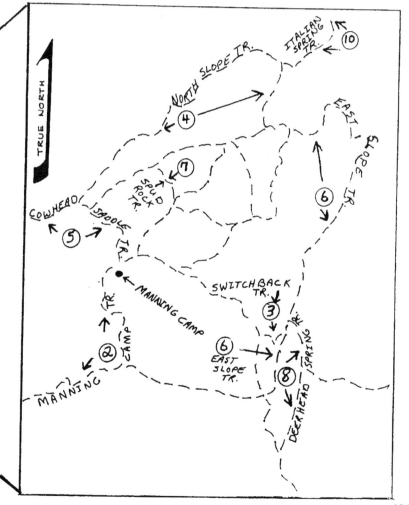

SANTA CATALINA MOUNTAINS TRAILS

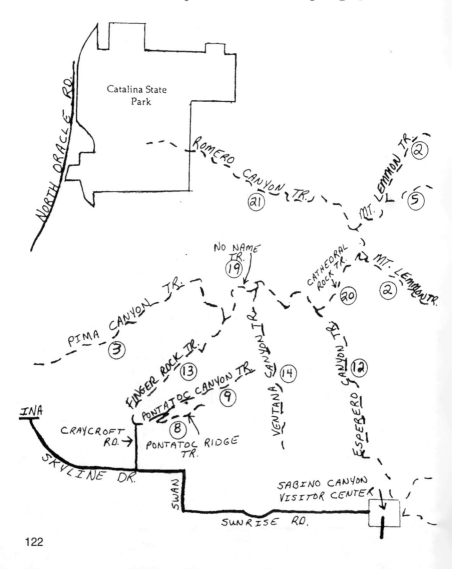

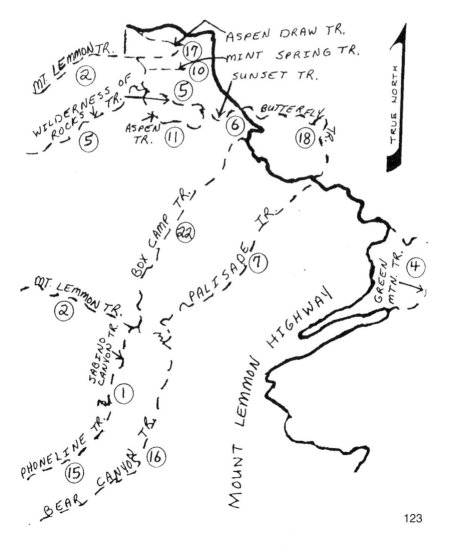

FOR ADDITIONAL INFORMATION ON THESE TRAILS

NORTH

Peaks Ranger District   **602-526-0866**
5075 North Highway 89   (pp. 12-22) Coconino County
Flagstaff, AZ 86004

Sedona Ranger District   **602-282-4119**
Box 300   (pp. 26-28) Coconino County
Sedona, AZ 86336

Verde Ranger District   **602-567-4121**
Box 670   (p. 30) Yavapai County
Camp Verde, AZ 86322

CENTRAL

City of Phoenix Parks, Rec. & Lib. Dept.   **602-262-4986**
2333 N. Central Ave.   (p. 33) Maricopa County
Phoenix, AZ 85004

Maricopa Parks & Recreation Dept.   **602-272-8871**
3475 W. Durango St.   (pp. 36-38) Maricopa County
Phoenix, AZ 85009

Bureau of Land Mgmt. (Safford Dist. Off.)   **602-428-4040**
425 E. 4th St.   (p. 41) Pinal County
Safford, AZ 85546

SOUTH

Organ Pipe National Monument   **602-387-6849**
Rt. 1, Box 100   (pp. 44-48) Pima County
Ajo, AZ 85321

Santa Catalina Ranger District   **602-749-8700**
5700 N. Sabino Canyon road   (pp. 50-88, 92) Pima County
Tucson, AZ 85715

Catalina State Park   **602-628-5798**
Box 36986   (p. 90) Pima County
Tucson, AZ 85740

Saguaro National Monument East   **602-296-8576**
3693 South Old Spanish Trail   (pp. 94-112) Pima County
Tucson, AZ 85730

Saguaro National Monument West   **602-883-6366**
2700 N. Kinney Road   (pp. 114-118) Pima County
Tucson, AZ 85743

TRAIL ETIQUETTE

Let's face it, if you meet someone on the trail, they are there to have a good time and get away from it all, the same as you. If everyone exercises courtesy and cooperation, then everyone has a better time.

Trail etiquette does not only mean using good manners toward other people, but also having respect for the trail itself and its signing.

Do not cut switchbacks on a trail, as it does cause erosion. Switchbacks are built to make a trail easier and cutting them only makes your hike harder.

Hiking up steep grades sometimes requires as much from you mentally as physically. Downhill hikers must always yield to hikers coming uphill, and do it in such a way as not to break their stride or concentration.

If you are hiking faster than the party ahead of you, slow down and wait for them to allow you to pass at an ideal location; thank them.

If you stop for a rest, do so well off the trail, in order to give others a clear path to travel. It is also easier for you not to be in their road.

Hiking or riding bikes on a wet trail ruins trails eventually, as well as cutting new trails to make shortcuts. We must respect the work that went into the original trail construction if we expect them to remain.

All trail users must yield to all trail stock. These animals are excitable, so remain calm and quiet as you allow them to pass. If these animals are panicked, a rider (or even you) could get badly hurt.

If you are allowed a pet on the trail, keep it on a leash. Be careful that you are clear of other hikers so as not to have the leash trip them.

The wilderness is a pristine, rewarding area if one will only take the time to enjoy it. I don't think anything messes it up more than loud noises or yelling for no reason.

If we all work together, we can make the great outdoors a pleasant place for everyone now, as well as in the future.

WEATHER-GREAT
BUT CHANGEABLE

The saying goes, "if you don't like the weather in Arizona, then just wait a few minutes."

This is a fine example of how fast a change can start to occur and, depending on how far you are out on the trail, and if unprepared, can be the start of your demise.

Arizona's wide array of extremes from the hot arid desert to the cool (if not freezing) lofty peaks carry with them the perfect ingredients for you to be concerned — concerned enough to insure that you never travel unprepared.

July and August are months that are most unpredictable, indeed. Storms gather quickly and drop a lot of water to cause real hazards in the deserts and mountains. Flash floods come in a flash and temperatures can drop severely in only minutes.

Winter rains in early spring are not to be taken lightly, either. As it is a colder time of the year, the dangers may be worse.

Check weather conditions and forecasts before you travel the trails. Many have lost their lives taking our deserts and mountains for granted.

Again I will stress, go prepared in every way you can, and be informed!

COPING WITH HYPOTHERMIA

Hypothermia is a condition that can set in when body heat is lost at a faster rate than your body can manufacture it.

One obvious place you may develop hypothermia is in water. Even though you are floating in a life preserver, it makes no difference. Even in 70 to 80 degree water, when exhausted, you will become unconscious in 3 to 12 hours. When in 32 degree water, the longest you would live would be 45 minutes.

In water is not the only place you can develop hypothermia, as you only need to get wet in rain, sleet, snow or heavy fog. Even perspiration, along with a moderately cool wind, can start the process. When you are wet in a moderate wind, a process the same as evaporative cooling will begin with no hope of your body keeping up.

More than half your body's heat is lost from your head and neck being exposed. Obviously, then, a good winter hat with ear tabs, along with a scarf, will do a lot to slow down your major heat loss.

Other susceptible areas are your hands and feet. It is a fact that mittens will keep your hands warmer than gloves, as the air around your hands will act as insulation. Waterproof boots will take care of your feet. Some rain gear only drapes your upper body and will soak your lower pant legs and boots. So, a better rain gear application is a two-piece coat and pants to relieve this problem.

If you find yourself in this situation, stop and make camp early and get a fire started, and try to create some cover. If you do this, you may not make it home that night and be overdue but, if you don't, you may not make it home at all. It's a small price to save your life.

It is most important to eat. Food will cause your body to develop heat from the digestion process. Fatty food, along with protein from meat or beans, creates a longer-lasting heat.

If someone in your group is showing signs of hypothermia, and you have made camp, get this person into dry clothes first of all and near your fire, if you have managed to start one. While this is being done, someone can be prewarming a sleeping bag, either at your fire or by lying down in it. Build an insulation barrier with leaves, etc., on which to lay the sleeping bag and keep him out of the wind. If the person is semi-conscious, give him warm drinks.

If the patient is going into severe hypothermia, then strip him and also yourself of clothing and get into the sleeping bag with this person, as there is no faster way to convey body heat. You have no other choice than to do this; it's almost a sure bet to save a life.

When headed to the mountains, think of hypothermia. When shopping for outdoor hiking gear, think hypothermia.

CONTENTS OF YOUR DAY PACK

Listed below are items I feel comfortable with. Feel free to add or subtract to suit your needs. Keep in mind that you may be planning a day hike that could turn into overnite for a variety of reasons. Again, go prepared!

1. Small flashlight, bulbs and batteries
2. Candies that will not melt or spoil
3. Whistle (a police whistle is ideal)
4. Good compass
5. Toilet paper
6. Complete first aid kit
7. Salt tablets
8. Strong sun screen
9. Any medicines or prescriptions you need
10. Pocket knife
11. Pencil and paper
12. Lighter and waterproof matches
13. Moleskin
14. Lip salve
15. Bug spray for body
16. One day extra food that will not spoil
17. Leakproof canteen and extra water
18. Enough clothing for possible overnight stay
19. Plastic bag for litter
20. Raingear
21. Hat
22. Gloves or mittens
23. Sunglasses
24. Maps
25. Camera and film
26. Identification

I will stress that your first aid kit and maps are valuable only if you study them very carefully **before** you leave.

If you do that and take along all of the above for your day hike, you can feel comfortable about your venture.

Let your friends or family know where you are going and when you expect to return and then stick to that plan so they can feel comfortable as well.

CONTENTS
OF YOUR BACKPACK

It is obvious that a day pack list is not ample by itself for multiple day outings. Nothing can ruin your outing quicker than an ill-fitting backpack. Make sure you get one large enough to fit perfectly. When satisfied with this, transfer everything from your day pack to your backpack and add the following (Again, these are things that I am comfortable with; pack to suit yourself.):

1. **Sleeping bag and bed roll.**
   Ask your supplier for help selecting this. Ask which is best for where you hike the most during time of year you hike.

2. **Tent.**
   Make sure your tent is portable and, above all, light-weight.

3. **Camping stove and extra fuel.**
   Buy a dependable product that is lightweight. It's easier than gathering wood. You are not permitted to build a wood fire in some areas.

4. **Permits.**
   By all means, pack needed permits so you can get to them easily.

Of course, all of the advice given you at the end of the Day Pack list also applies again here.

SAFETY RULES
FOR SURVIVAL IN THE DESERT

(Courtesy Maricopa County Civil Defense and Emergency Services)

1. Never go into the desert without first informing someone as to your destination, your route and when you will return. STICK TO YOUR PLAN.

2. Carry at least one gallon of water per person per day of your trip. Plastic jugs are handy and portable.

3. Be sure your vehicle is in good condition.

4. KEEP AN EYE ON THE SKY. Flash floods may occur any time "thunder-heads" are in sight, even though it may not rain where you are.

5. If your vehicle breaks down, stay near it. Your emergency supplies are here. Raise your hood and trunk lid to denote "Help Needed"

6. If you are POSITIVE of the route to help, and must leave your vehicle, leave a note for rescuers as to when you left and the direction you are taking.

7. If you have water — DRINK IT. Do not ration it.

8. If water is limited — KEEP YOUR MOUTH SHUT. Do not talk, do not eat, do not smoke, do not drink alcohol, do not take salt.

9. Do not sit or lie DIRECTLY on the ground. It may be 30 degrees or more hotter than the air.

10. A roadway is a sign of civilization. IF YOU FIND A ROAD, STAY ON IT.

The Desert Southwest is characterized by brilliant sunshine, a wide temperature range, sparse vegetation, a scarcity of water, a high rate of evaporation and low annual rainfall.

Travel in the desert can be an interesting and enjoyable experience or it can be a fatal or near fatal nightmare. The contents of this manual can give only a few of the details necessary for full enjoyment of our desert out-of-doors.

If you think you are lost, do not panic. Sit down for a while, survey the area and take stock of the situation. Try to remember how long it has been since you knew where you were. Decide on a course of action. It may be best to stay right where you are and let your companions or rescuers look for you. This is especially true if there is water and fuel nearby or if there is some means of shelter. Once you decide to remain, make a fire — a smoky one for daytime and a bright one for the night. Other signals may be used, but fire is by far the best.

REMEMBER, MOVE WITH A PURPOSE, NEVER START OUT AND WANDER AIMLESSLY.

Walking: There are special rules and techniques for walking in the desert. By walking slowly and resting about 10 minutes per hour a man in good physical condition can cover about 12-18 miles per day — less after he becomes fatigued or lacks sufficient water or food. On the hot desert it is best to travel early morning or late evening, spending mid-day in whatever shade may be available. In walking, pick the easiest and safest way. Go around obstacles, not over them. Instead of going up or down steep slopes, zigzag to prevent undue exertion. Go around gullies and canyons instead of through them. When walking with companions, adjust the rate to the slowest man. Keep together but allow about 10 feet between members.

At rest stops, if you can sit down in the shade and prop your feet up, remove your shoes and change socks, or straighten out the ones you are wearing. If the ground is too hot to sit on, no shade is available, and you cannot raise your feet, do not remove your shoes as you may not be able to get them back onto swollen feet.

Automobile Driving: Cross country driving or driving on little used roads is hazardous, but can be done successfully if a few simple rules are followed. Move slowly. Do not attempt to negotiate washes without first checking the footing and the clearances. High centers may rupture the oil pan. Overhang may cause the driving wheels to become suspended above the ground. Do not spin wheels in an attempt to gain motion, but apply power very slowly to prevent wheel spin and subsequent digging in. When driving in sand, traction can be increased by partially deflating tires. Start, stop and turn gradually, as sudden motions cause wheels to dig in. There are certain tool and equipment requirements if you intend to drive off the main roads: a shovel, a pick-mattock, a tow chain or cable, at least 50 feet of strong tow rope, tire pump, axe, water cans, gas cans, and of course, your regular spare parts and auto tools.

Clothing: For the desert, light-weight and light colored clothing which covers the whole body is best. Long trousers and long sleeves protect from the sun, help to prevent dehydration and protect against insects, abrasions and lacerations by rocks and brush. Headgear should provide all-around shade as well as eye shade.

Survival Kit: Items that should be carried on the individual are: a sharp knife, a signal mirror, a map of the area, thirty or more feet of nylon string, canteen, matches, a snake bite kit, a firearm and ammunition, and other items that may be useful. Consider carrying your gear in a small rucksack or pack over your shoulders. Weight carried in this manner is less tiring than if carried in pockets or hung on the belt. The pack can be used to sit upon. It also affords a safer method of carrying items, such as the belt knife, hatchet, etc., which may lend to the chances of injury in case of a fall.

Health Hazards: Thought must be given to protecting your health and well-being, and the prevention of fatigue and injury: first, because medical assistance will be some distance away; second, because conditions are usually different and distinct from your everyday living. The desert is a usually healthy environment due to dryness, the lack of human and animal wastes, and the sterilizing effect of the hot sun. Therefore, your immediate bodily needs will be your first consideration.

If you are walking or active, rest 10 minutes each hour. Drink plenty of water, especially early in the morning while the temperature is still low.

While in the desert, wear sun glasses to protect your eyes from glare. Even though the glare does not seem to bother you, it will impair your distant vision and will retard your adaptation to night conditions. If you have no glasses make an eyeshade by slitting a piece of paper, cardboard or cloth. Applying charcoal or soot around the eyes is also beneficial.

In a survival situation everything that you do, each motion that you make, and each step you take must be preceded by the thought: am I safe in doing this?

Keep your clothing on, including shirt and hat. Clothing helps ration your sweat by slowing the evaporation rate and prolonging the cooling effect. It also keeps out the hot desert air and reflects the heat of the sun.

Rationing water at high temperatures is actually inviting disaster because small amounts will not prevent dehydration. Loss of efficiency and collapse always follows dehydration. It is the water in your body that maintains your life, not the water in your canteen.

Keep the mouth shut and breathe through the nose to reduce water loss and drying of mucous membranes. Avoid conversation for the same reason. If possible, cover lips with grease or oil. Alcohol in any form is to be avoided as it will accelerate dehydration. Consider alcohol as food and not as water since additional water is required to assimilate the alcohol. For the same reason, food intake should be kept to a minimum if sufficient water is not available.

Carrying Water: When planning to travel, give your water supply extra thought. Do not carry water in glass containers as these may break. Metal insulated containers are good, but heavy. Carry some water in gallon or half-gallon plastic containers similar to those containing bleach. They are unbreakable, light-weight and carrying several will assure a water supply if one is damaged.

Finding Water in the Desert: If you are near water it is best to remain there and prepare signals for your rescuers. If no water is immediately available look for it, following these leads:

Watch for desert trails — following them may lead to water or civilization, particularly if several such trails join and point toward a specific location.

Flocks of birds will circle over water holes. Listen for their chirping in the morning and evening, and you may be able to locate their watering spot. Quail move toward water in the late afternoon and away in the morning. Doves flock toward watering spots morning and evening. Also look for indications of animals as they tend to feed near water.

Look for plants which grow only where there is water: cottonwoods, sycamores, willows, hackberry, saltcedar, cattails and arrow weed. You may have to dig to find this water. Also keep on the lookout for windmills and water tanks built by ranchers. If cactus fruits are ripe, eat a lot of them to help prevent dehydration.

Methods of Purifying Water: Dirty water should be filtered through several layers of cloth or allowed to settle. This does not purify the water even though it may look clean. Purification to kill germs must be done by one of the following methods:

1. Water purification tablets are the easiest to use. Get them from the drug store and follow the directions on the label. Let stand for thirty minutes.

2. Tincture of Iodine: add three drops per quart of clear water, double for cloudy water. Let stand for thirty minutes.

3. Boiling for 3 to 5 minutes will purify most water.

Food: You must have water to survive, but you can go without food for a few days without harmful effects. In fact, if water is not available, do not eat, as food will only increase your need for water. The important thing about locating food in a survival situation is to know what foods are available in the particular invironment and how to obtain them. Hawks soaring overhead may mean water is nearby. Game will be found around water holes and areas that have heavy brush growth.

Edible Wildlife: Almost every animal, reptile and insect is edible. Learn how to prepare the various things that would be available to you in a survival situation. Avoid any small mammal which appears to be sick. Some animals have scent glands which must be removed before cooking. Do not allow the animal hair to come in contact with the flesh as it will give the meat a disagreeable taste.

1. Jack Rabbit: A hare, with long ears and legs, sandy color. Grubs are often found in the hide or flesh but these do not affect the food value.

2. Cottontail Rabbit: Small, pale gray with white tail. Active in the early morning and late evening.

3. Javelina: Dark gray-black, weighing 30-50 pounds with strong tusks. Has scent glands on the back, over the hind legs. May be dangerous if cornered or wounded.

4. Mourning Dove: Year-round resident, usually found near habitation and water.

5. Gambel's Quail, Scaled Quail, Mearn's Quail: The Gambel's is of primary importance in desert and semi-arid areas.

6. Snakes: Most snakes are edible. Rattlesnake is especially good.

7. Desert Tortoise.

Edible Plants: The main desert edibles are the fruits of the cacti and legumes. All cactus fruits are safe to eat. In the summer the fleshy and thin-walled ripe fruits can be singed over a fire to remove spines. Then they can be peeled and eaten. Old cactus fruits contain seeds which can be pounded between two stones into a powder and eaten, or mixed with water into a gruel. New, young pads of the prickly pear can be singed, peeled and boiled.

The legumes are the bean bearing plants. The main ones are the mesquite, the palo verde, the ironwood and the catclaw. All are small trees with fern-like leaves. All have bean pods which when green and tender can be boiled and eaten. Dry, mature beans, like cactus seeds, are too hard to chew and must be cooked.

In a survival situation, where the use of strange plants for food is indicated, follow these rules: Avoid plants with milky sap. Avoid all red beans. If possible, boil plants which are questionable. Test a cooked plant by holding a small quantity in the mouth for a few moments. If the taste is disagreeable, do not eat it.

Fires and Cooking: Clear an area about 15 feet across, dig a pit or arrange rocks to contain the fire. Make a starting fire of dry grass, small twigs, shavings, under-bark of cottonwoods, etc. Place larger twigs — about pencil size — on top. Have heavier material ready to add, using the small pieces first. Place them on the fire in a "tepee" fashion to prevent smothering your starting fire and aid in the formation of an up-draft. After the fire is burning well, continue to use the tepee method for boiling but criss-cross fuel for forming coals for frying or broiling.

Start your fire with a lighter, matches, or a hand lens. Remember, do not use up your water-proofed matches unless your return from the field is a guaranteed fact. Here are some hints for expeditious fire building.

Drying matches: Damp wooden matches can be dried by stroking 20 to 30 times through the dry hair at the side of the head. Be careful not to knock off the chemical head of very wet matches at the start of the procedure.

Tinder: (All of these must be dry.) Under-bark of the cottonwood, cedar bark, dead goldenrod tops, cattail floss, charred cloth, bird nests, mouse nests, or any readily flammable material shredded into fine fibers.

Fuzz-stick: Cut slivers into soft wood sticks and arrange them tepee fashion with the separated ends downward.

Quick, hot fires: Cottonwood, cactus skeletons, creosote-bush, aspen, tamarisk, cedar, pine, and spruce.

Long-lasting fires: Mesquite, ironwood, black jack, sage, and oak.

REMEMBER, YOU WANT FLAME FOR HEAT, EMBERS FOR COOKING, AND FOR SIGNALS YOU NEED SMOKE IN THE DAYTIME AND BRIGHT FIRES AT NIGHT. BE SURE TO EXTINGUISH YOUR FIRE BEFORE LEAVING IT!

Poisonous Creatures: There is probably more said and less truth about poisonous creatures than any other subject. These animals and insects are for the most part shy, or due to their nature, not often seen. Learn the facts about these creatures and you will see that they are not to be feared but only respected.

Snakes: There are many types of snakes in the southwest but only rattlesnakes and coral snakes are poisonous. Snakes hibernate during the colder months, but will start appearing with the warming trend, sometimes in early February. During the spring and fall months they may be found out in the daytime, but during the summer months they will generally be found out during the night, due to the fact that they cannot stand excessive heat.

Rattlesnakes: These are easily identified by the sandy color, the broad arrow-shaped head, blunt tipped-up nose, and rattles on the tail. Look for them mostly where food, water, and protection is available — around abandoned structures, irrigation ditches, water holes, brush and rock piles. They do not always give warning by rattling, nor do they always strike if one is close. If travelling in areas where rattlers are, wear protective footgear and watch where you put your hands and feet.

Arizona Coral Snake: A small snake, rarely over 20 inches long with small blunt, black head and tapering tail. Wide red and black bands are separated by narrower yellow bands and all completely encircle the body. They are noctunal and live under objects, in burrows, and are shy and timid. Corals bite and chew rather than strike, but due to the very small mouth they are unable to bite any but the smallest extremities.

Treatment of Poisonous Snakebite: If bitten, try to capture the snake as identification will aid in specific medical treatment.

1. KEEP THE VICTIM QUIET AND SEEK MEDICAL HELP.

2. If the "cut and suck" method is deemed necessary, follow the instructions with the snake bite kit. In any event, step 1 above, is very important.

Poisonous Insects and Spiders: The potentially lethal species in this area are the scorpion and the black widow spider.

Prevention and Treatment: In places where venomous species are expected, inspect all clothing and bedding before use, especially items that have been on or near the ground. If bitten (stung), get to a doctor, especially if the victim is a child, is elderly, has a bad heart, or has been bitten several times or on the main part of the body.

WHAT TO DO
WHEN LOST IN THE WOODS

You might think food, water, proper clothing, or even being attacked by a wild animal, are the most important things with which you had better concern yourself if you are lost in the wilderness.

However, all of the above are secondary or even immaterial if you do not exercise calmness and keep a clear head. If you allow yourself to panic then, indeed, you are lost and will probably only be found by accident. Just because you cannot see a trail or a familiar sight does not mean you cannot find your way back. Understandably, this situation can instill fear but, above all, do not give in to it.

If you find yourself in this situation, do not wander about. Rather, sit down, calm yourself and very carefully try to run through in your mind the events that led up to your getting lost. Instead of letting your feet do the work, use a clear mind.

If you fail to figure out what went wrong and you still have plenty of daylight left, and want to travel slowly, then do so. Make sure, however, that if you had been climbing, you now only travel downhill.

If you come to a stream, do not ever leave it unless, of course, you have found your way. A stream can almost always supply you with water and food, and usually leads to civilization, as well.

Keep a very close eye on the daylight you have left and remember it gets dark earlier on the backside of a mountain away from the sun. If your daylight will soon be gone and you are still lost, you should immediately find a place to camp overnight. Gather whatever rocks or stones are available, place them in a circle to make a place for a safe fire, and gather some wood. You should have a fire burning by dark. Also by the time it's dark, you should have eaten if you have food. You must know where everything in your camp is by then.

If you cannot build a fire because you have no dry

firewood, and you do not have a blanket or bedroll, then cover yourself with sticks and leaves to escape the cold and wind; it works.

If you are injured and cannot travel, then a signal fire is your best bet, of course, using enough common sense not to start a forest fire. A very smoky fire by day and a bright fire at night has the best chance of bringing results.

You can now see how important a fishing line, compass, map, matches and a good knife are in a situation like this, as well as the rest of the supplies that are listed elsewhere in this book. You must always enter the woods prepared, even for the possibility of getting lost.

A situation such as this, before you turn in for the night, may seem hopeless, but can take on a brighter outlook in the morning when again your head is clear.

At the risk of repeating myself, all of the information I have given you so far is useless if you are not going to stay calm and use your head. It has been proven over and over that a clear head will get you out.

WHAT TO WEAR
FOR MOUNTAIN HIKING

In the "Desert Survival" chapter in this book are hints on proper dress for the desert, but mountain dress has a different application. Mountain dress has its variables for lower rolling hills or higher rugged peaks.

LOWER ROLLING HILLS

In these gentle areas, one can use with great comfort the lightweight hiking boots that are popular today. It's not too likely you will need extreme support for lower elevations. Most of these hikes are one-day outings or shorter, so a heavy backpack need not be carried. Lightweight boots will not support a heavy pack.

Hiking shorts or denim pants work well here, as it is not likely to be cold. I prefer long sleeves and a hat to prevent sunburn. A day pack works well on shorter hikes of this nature. Sweat shirt and raingear are a must.

HIGHER RUGGED PEAKS

In this kind of hiking one must have a very rugged hiking boot, not only for traction, but also the ever-present need for good support. Some hikers even buy their boots a half size too large, making room for two pair of socks for more comfort. If you do not buy waterproof boots, then at least spray them with products available to treat them to repel water. These kinds of boots also will support a heavy pack as well as provide comfort.

Again, denim jeans wear well but do not provide much warmth in extreme cold. If you do not wear them hiking, then you might consider carrying in your backpack warmer pants and longjohns for the other conditions. T-shirts are most comfortable under your outer shirts. As you notice, I said "shirts." I do find wearing a couple of shirts instead of one heavy one makes it easier to adjust one's temperature by wearing only what is needed instead of too much or too little.

A warm hat, scarf and mittens should also be carried on these hikes. On mountain hiking, a backpack is needed to carry all necessary supplies. Have the people where you buy your backpack spend some time to insure a proper fit. A backpack is like a boot. It must fit.

Although maybe not worn during hiking, a heavy jacket can be quite an asset when camping or just resting for a while. It is better to be prepared for the worst than to be caught without.

Index

About the Author

Cave manager and explorer, writer, hiker, pilot, trail blazer and back-country ranger, Don Kiefer is a man in love with his work. To date he has logged more than 3400 miles hiking in Arizona.

He started writing for the *Mesa Tribune* about seven years ago, and has subsequently written for four papers. Through that experience he bagan working for Colossal Cave Mountain Park, starting as a tour guide and working into management.

Don's first book, **Hiking Arizona**, now in its third printing, was just the beginning of an entire series of hiking books about Arizona trails. He is currently working on several new volumes featuring hiking trails throughout the state.

Don has been cited by the United States Forest Service for his assistance with historical research and in 1991 he received the Presidential Sports Award from President George Bush. Don has also performed service for theArizona State Parks and the National Forest Service.

About the Artist

Robyn Wasserman is currently employed by Arizona State Parks. She has been a hiking guide, naturalist, forestry technician and fire dispatcher.

Outdoor Books from Golden West Publishers

HIKING ARIZONA

) hiking trails throughout this beautiful state. Desert safety—what
 wear, what to take, what to do if lost. Each hike has a detailed map,
king time, distance, difficulty, elevation, attractions, etc. Perfect
r novice or experienced hikers. *Hiking Arizona* by Don R. Kiefer.

5 1/2 x 8 1/2— 160 pages . . . $6.95

EXPLORE ARIZONA!

here to find old coins, bottles, fossil beds, arrowheads, petro-
yphs, waterfalls, ice caves, cliff dwellings. Detailed maps to 59
izona wonders! *Explore Arizona!* by Rick Harris.

5 1/2 x 8 1/2— 128 pages . . . $6.95

DISCOVER ARIZONA!

joy the thrill of discovery! Prehistoric ruins, caves, historic
ttlegrounds, fossil beds, arrowheads, waterfalls, rock crystals and
mi-precious stones! *Discover Arizona!* by Rick Harris.

5 1/2 x 8 1/2—112 pages . . . $6.95

VERDE RIVER RECREATION GUIDE

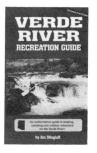

ide to Arizona's Verde River and its tributaries, section by
tion. For boaters, campers, hikers, tubers, naturalists. Includes
es of water to be encountered, surrounding terrain, wildlife. Plus
mping and boating advice, whitewater ratings, maps, photos,
ex. *Verde River Recreation Guide* by Jim Slingluff.

5 1/2 x 8 1/2—176 pages . . . $6.95

ARIZONA MUSEUMS

mplete listings for more than 200 Arizona archaeological parks,
 centers, botanical gardens, museums and zoos. Each listing
cludes: name, address, directions, phone, days open, hours, and
tailed descriptions of the collections, the highlights and the
ecial exhibits.

5 1/2 x 8 1/2—240 pages . . . $9.95

ORDER BLANK

GOLDEN WEST PUBLISHERS

☀ 4113 N. Longview Ave. • Phoenix, AZ 85014

602-265-4392 • **1-800-658-5830** • FAX 602-279-6901

Qty	Title	Price	Amount
	Arizona Cook Book	5.95	
	Arizona Crosswords	4.95	
	Arizona Museums	9.95	
	Arizona—Off the Beaten Path	5.95	
	Arizona Outdoor Guide	5.95	
	Arizona Small Game & Fish Recipes	5.95	
	Cactus Country	6.95	
	Chili Lovers Cook Book	5.95	
	Cowboy Slang	5.95	
	Discover Arizona!	6.95	
	Explore Arizona!	6.95	
	Fishing Arizona	7.95	
	Ghost Towns in Arizona	5.95	
	Hiking Arizona	6.95	
	Hiking Arizona II	6.95	
	Quest for the Dutchman's Gold	6.95	
	Snakes and other Reptiles of the SW	9.95	
	Verde River Recreation Guide	6.95	
	Wild West Characters	6.95	
Add $2.00 to total order for shipping & handling			**$2.00**

☐ My Check or Money Order Enclosed. . . . . $

☐ MasterCard ☐ VISA

Acct. No.   Exp. Date

Signature

Name   Telephone

Address

City/State/Zip

Call for FREE catalog

Hiking II

4/93   **MasterCard and VISA Orders Accepted ($20 Minimum)**

This order blank may be photo-copied.